Cheryl Hazeltine's
Central Texas
Gardener

NUMBER FORTY-FIVE
Louise Lindsey Merrick Natural
History Series

Cheryl Hazeltine's

Central Texas Gardener

Cheryl Hazeltine

Photographs by Cheryl Hazeltine & Richard Hazeltine

TEXAS A&M UNIVERSITY PRESS • COLLEGE STATION

LIBRARY OF CONGRESS CATALOGING-
IN-PUBLICATION DATA

   Hazeltine, Cheryl, 1942–
[Central Texas gardener]
Cheryl Hazeltine's central Texas
gardener / Cheryl Hazeltine.—1st ed.
        p. cm.—(Louise Lindsey Merrick
Natural History Series; no. 45)
Central Texas gardener
Previously published in 1980 as The
central Texas gardener and in 1999 as
The new central Texas gardener.
  Includes index.
  ISBN-13: 978–1-60344–206–0
(flexibound : alk. paper)
  ISBN-10: 1–60344–206–5
(flexibound : alk. paper)
  1. Gardening—Texas.   I. Hazeltine,
Cheryl, 1942- New central Texas gardener.
II. Title.
SB453.2.T4H39   2010
635.09764—dc22
2010003598

For Ira & Ridley

Contents

Preface

In the last twenty years, gardening in Central Texas has been through many changes, from minor cultural practices to broad and deep attitudinal and philosophical reconsiderations. So many positive changes have done much to expand the gardener's knowledge and pleasure.

Thanks to soil researchers like Elaine Ingham at Oregon State University and others, care of the soil has become the safekeeping of the garden's soul. Gardeners who once limited discussion of fertilizer to the merits of N-P-K ratios now extol the role of mycorrhizal fungi and other microbes in plant nutrition and disease control. Compost tumblers and compost tea brewers are for sale everywhere.

In design, the broad, uninterrupted lawn and house with mustache-planted (straight across the foundation) evergreen shrubs have given way to more imaginative and interesting scenes of curb and island gardens and well-placed architectural accent plants. Ponds and water features are in gardens great and small. Even the lonely potted geranium has morphed into a container garden of grasses, vines, and flowers. Twenty years ago it was impossible to imagine Texas Parks and Wildlife Department teaming up with the National Wildlife Foundation to promote "Best of Texas Backyard Habitats" certification.

Today native plants have a secure place in local nurseries and even big-box stores. Cultivars of *Salvia greggii* are almost as numerous as petunias. Many younger or newer gardeners may not even be aware these are natives. Sago palms and aloes, once considered container plants to be overwintered indoors, now have their roots in the landscape.

As regional growth in the residential, industrial, and agricultural sectors has put greater pressure on our water resources, mandatory watering schedules have become the rule rather than the exception. "Xeriscape," "water-wise," whatever name we apply, water conservation must be practiced by all.

Always there but not in the mainstream, organic gardening has made a move to front and center as consumers hear more frequently about tainted crop recalls and pesticide removals from the market.

This book seeks to blend the best of the traditional with a focus on the new, including new ways we seek and use information. The current emphasis on working with nature presents an opportunity for Central Texas gardeners to learn about and enjoy the challenges and possibilities of where they live.

Acknowledgments

Gardening is a continuous learning experience. We learn from many sources, but above all we learn from our gardens and our fellow gardeners.

More than thirty years ago Joan (Filvaroff) Bailin suggested that she and I write a badly needed garden book for Central Texas. I was at first reluctant, but Joan persisted. As a result, *The Central Texas Gardener* was published by Texas A&M University Press. Ten years ago, friend and neighbor Barry Lovelace said the book needed an update and offered to join me. Together we wrote *The New Central Texas Gardener*. Both voices echo loudly throughout this new work, and I am indebted to them always.

I wish to thank Barbara Gamble for introducing me to the wonderful world of Sunshine Community Garden (SCG) in Austin; Susan Hoberman, whose confident and intrepid gardening is always helpful and inspiring; Vernon Barker, Ila Falvey, Margaret Powis, and Nancy Seibert, who so love the garden and never fail to bring experience and perspective to the discussion.

I wish to thank Kay Kitzmiller, my co-gardener on the "Hazeltine-Kitzmiller Farms" plot at SCG. Kay, who taught me to like vegetables, has enriched our shared gardening experience with her broad mastery and love of cooking and so much more; George Kitzmiller, who is always at the ready to improve infrastructure; Betsy Pobanz, for generously sharing her knowledge and love of native plants; and Diana Tilley, for boundless generosity and her unfailing attention.

I am ever so grateful to Shannon Davies, editor extraordinaire at Texas A&M University Press, whose patience, encouragement, support, and contributions have made so much possible through the years. Last, I thank Richard Hazeltine, my husband, ever-willing photographer, patient adviser, and lifelong mentor and supporter.

Cheryl Hazeltine's
Central Texas
Gardener

CHAPTER 1

Where We Live

THE NINETY-eighth meridian slices through Central Texas, just west of Waco and Austin and a little to the east of San Antonio. Noted Texas historian Walter Prescott Webb writes that in the settlement of our country this imaginary line marked the change from the timbered and well-watered East to the treeless, arid West. Here lies the 30-inch rainfall line where oaks and other hardwoods begin to give way to mesquite. Confronted with a new climate, new flora and fauna and land characteristics, those who settled here were forced to change their ways of farming, their tools, and even their laws governing land and water use to survive.

Today people continue to come to Central Texas from many regions and countries; many

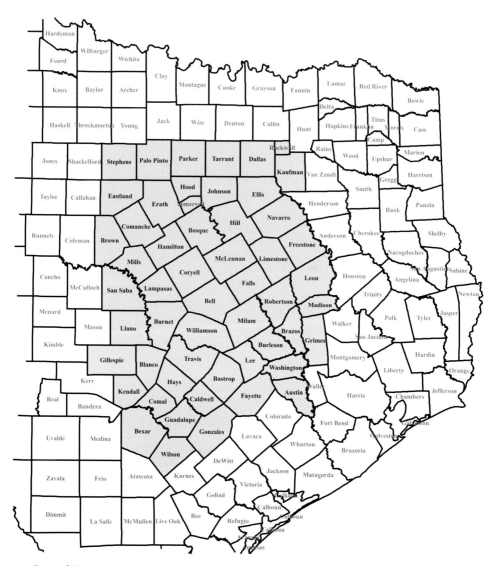

Central Texas

newcomers want to garden, if not to farm. To succeed, they, like the settlers of long ago, must learn to deal with erratic rainfall, searing heat, large and rapid temperature changes, and difficult soil. In spite of the challenges, opportunities abound. We can garden year-round, and with knowledge, care, and luck we can grow a variety of plants from the temperate to tropical zones.

Successful gardening begins with selecting the right plant for the right place. In the less forgiving Central Texas environment, that requires an understanding of climate and soil and learning as much as possible about the plants' growing requirements. Fortunately, numerous excellent resources—print, media, and the Internet—make gathering information about plants easier than ever. We can do a lot of tweaking in the garden, for example, amending or even importing soil, or planting in containers, to expand our choices and accommodate specialty plants, but the good fit of plant to location is the basis of a thriving garden or landscape.

Central Texas Climate

Climate is weather over the long haul. Central Texas has a modified subtropical climate. Our long growing season ranges from 230 to 275 days. From May through September warm, humid, tropical air breezes in from the Gulf of Mexico, bringing us the glorious cumulus clouds of summer and the troublesome thunderstorms that delay our flights into and out of DFW airport. As we go west of Interstate 35, into the Hill Country, the air becomes more arid. Hail, flash floods, and tornados are not uncommon.

Our summers (roughly April through October) are long and hot. The area has about 111 days when the temperature exceeds 90°F! At night, clouds roll in and trap the heat and humidity; temperatures rarely fall below 73°F. It is the unrelenting nature of the heat that sets us apart from other hot areas (Wichita, Kansas; Albuquerque, New Mexico; Sacramento, California) where nighttime temperatures drop significantly lower. In Central Texas, neither the plants nor we get a chance to cool off.

In winter (November through March), temperatures can be more variable. And when the changes come, they can come very quickly. "Blue Northers" sweep down off the plains, dropping temperatures as much as 40°F in a few hours, freezing

4

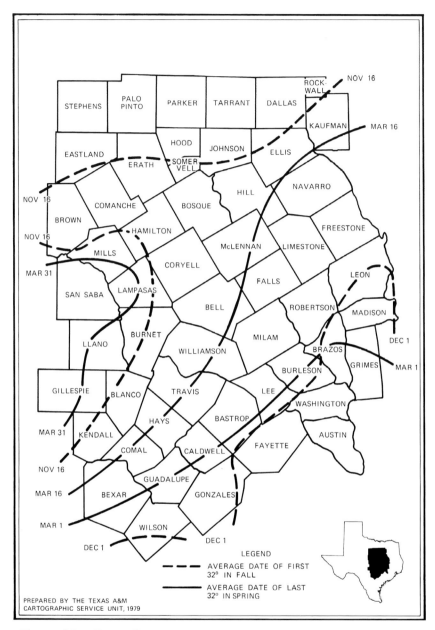

First and Last Freeze Dates

Map labels: STEPHENS, PALO PINTO, PARKER, TARRANT, DALLAS, ROCK-WALL, NOV 16, KAUFMAN, MAR 16, EASTLAND, HOOD, JOHNSON, ELLIS, ERATH, SOMER-VELL, HILL, NAVARRO, NOV 16, COMANCHE, BOSQUE, BROWN, FREESTONE, NOV 16, HAMILTON, MILLS, McLENNAN, LIMESTONE, MAR 31, CORYELL, LEON, SAN SABA, LAMPASAS, FALLS, BELL, ROBERTSON, MADISON, BURNET, MILAM, DEC 1, LLANO, WILLIAMSON, BRAZOS, GRIMES, MAR 1, BURLESON, GILLESPIE, BLANCO, TRAVIS, LEE, WASHINGTON, HAYS, BASTROP, AUSTIN, MAR 31, KENDALL, COMAL, CALDWELL, FAYETTE, NOV 16, MAR 16, BEXAR, GUADALUPE, GONZALES, MAR 1, WILSON, DEC 1, DEC 1

LEGEND
— — — AVERAGE DATE OF FIRST 32° IN FALL
———— AVERAGE DATE OF LAST 32° IN SPRING

PREPARED BY THE TEXAS A&M
CARTOGRAPHIC SERVICE UNIT, 1979

Differences between 1990 USDA hardiness zones and 2006 arborday.org hardiness zones reflect warmer climate

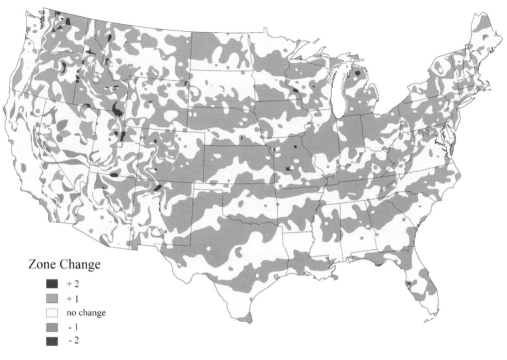

Zone Change

- + 2
- + 1
- no change
- - 1
- - 2

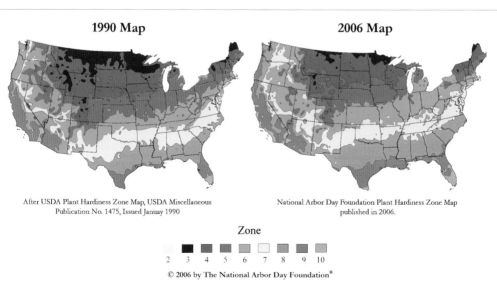

1990 Map

After USDA Plant Hardiness Zone Map, USDA Miscellaneous Publication No. 1475, Issued Januay 1990

2006 Map

National Arbor Day Foundation Plant Hardiness Zone Map published in 2006.

Zone

2 3 4 5 6 7 8 9 10

Hardiness Zone Maps

unsuspecting tomatoes on the vine, and wiping out the last stand of summer annuals. Again, hail, torrential rains, and damaging winds may accompany these sudden weather changes.

Microclimates are small pockets in which the climate conditions differ from those of the larger, surrounding area. Human-made structures or naturally occurring features such as slopes or bodies of water may create these areas. They need to be considered in landscape plans. Frequently they offer protection and opportunities for plants that just would not survive out in the open, such as a Japanese maple in the protection of a courtyard.

We know our climate is changing. We don't know how quickly, where, and how. But it has changed enough over the past two decades that the U.S. Department of Agriculture (USDA) has updated its Hardiness Zone Map to reflect those changes. Major areas of the United States have been shifted to one zone warmer; other areas, two zones.

When rain comes, how fast it falls is as important as how much. Seasons interrupted by freak cold snaps or heat spells play havoc with plant metabolism and pest life cycles. Interesting times.

How Plants Work, and Why Climate and Weather Matter

It is hard to overestimate how truly remarkable plants are. We seldom consider how dependent upon them we are. Using the sun's energy, they are able to produce their own food. We, on the other hand, must eat plants or the flesh of animals that have eaten plants. Plants also contribute oxygen, a by-product of photosynthesis, to the air we breathe. Little wonder that Robert De Feo, chief horticulturist for the National Park Service, thinks photosynthesis is the most important chemical reaction on earth.

Following is a brief summary of the three major functions responsible for plant growth and development:

1. Photosynthesis (produces food, stores energy, releases oxygen, uses water and carbon dioxide, occurs in sunlight)
2. Respiration (uses food, releases energy, uses oxygen, produces carbon dioxide, occurs in light or dark)
3. Transpiration (transports minerals from the soil and cools plants, using up to 90 percent of water taken up by roots)

These processes depend on light, temperature, water—in a word, weather—and nutrients (nutrients and soil are the subject of the next chapter). Having evolved in different locations and under varying conditions, plants have developed different survival strategies. Two obvious examples are the large, broad leaves of jungle understory plants that collect as much sunlight as possible; and the tiny, tough, often gray leaves of desert plants that reflect light.

Light

Plants respond to duration, color, and quantity of light. Sunlight is required for photosynthesis; it also heats things up. Latitude and elevation are also factors in how plants respond to light. The duration and intensity of light change in our gardens as the seasons go forward. Before we embark on major, permanent planting, we should determine how the sun strikes the garden each season. Deciduous trees may open up previously shaded areas for fall and winter annuals, or long shadows may eliminate the possibility of a fall vegetable garden. Plant tags that say "full sun to part shade" tell only part of the story. What is "part sun"?

PROTECTING PLANTS FROM SUMMER'S HEAT

- Select plants that can take Central Texas heat.
- Water appropriately according to plants' requirements.
- Get new plants in the ground before the heat arrives.
- Use shade cloth to protect new transplants.
- Do not spray chemicals on plants when temperatures rise above 90°F.
- Mulch.

Filtered light, bright sun part of the day, and total shade during another part? A half day of afternoon sun in summer is very different from a half day of morning sun. For many of the more tender flowers morning sun is a blessing. Save the baking afternoon sun for the hardy sun lovers.

Temperature

Temperature is a major factor in plant growth and productivity. If temperatures are too low or too high, vegetables will fail to set fruit, growth will be stunted, and flavor may be affected. Certain bulbs will not bloom if they are not given a chilling period in the refrigerator. Seedlings have lower optimum temperatures than more mature plants of the same species.

Photosynthesis and respiration both increase as the temperature rises until about 90°F, when respiration continues to rise but photosynthesis plateaus. When plants use more food than they are creating, growth stops. Ideally, plants grow best when daytime temperatures are 10° to 15° higher than nighttime temperatures.

PROTECTING PLANTS
AGAINST THE COLD

- Plant tropicals and other tender plants in containers, which can be brought inside.
- Plant in a protected location, close to a fence or wall for wind protection.
- Water well before a cold front arrives.
- For short-term protection, wrap in cloth or other insulating material. Do not use plastic directly on plants because it conducts cold.
- Protect vulnerable vegetables with row cover.

Water

Heat, periods of low humidity, and wind all increase the rates of evaporation and transpiration, causing plants to lose moisture. Water is the environmental factor that is most easily in our control—turn on the sprinkler. Statistically, April, May, and June are our wettest months, with September often spilling rain from dissipating tropical storms. Our modest annual rainfall of 3 inches is often delivered in torrential downpours, overwhelming soil-holding capacity and causing heavy runoff. Then there are years the rains don't seem to come at all. Recent population growth and development have put additional pressure on water supplies. It is our responsibility as homeowners and gardeners to include water conservation practices in our gardens and landscape plans.

Water Conservation—a Part of Every Landscape and Garden Plan

Landscape and gardens account for 25 percent of water use in urban areas of Texas. In 1978, Xeriscape, copyrighted by the City of Denver Water Department, was the first widespread program to encourage water conservation in the home landscape. Today, water conservation programs like WaterWise and Austin's Grow Green program have official support and commercial partners in Central Texas. These programs offer excellent advice on design, plant selection, water-saving tips, and appropriate chemical use. With careful planning, wise plant selection, and proper care our gardens and landscapes will flourish. Most current programs are based on Xeriscape principles.

XERISCAPE PRINCIPLES

- Start with a good design or plan.
- Improve the soil. Almost all Central Texas soil can be improved by the addition of organic matter, which, among other things, aids in retention of soil moisture.
- Use mulch. Mulches discourage weeds, keep soil temperature lower, and improve moisture retention.
- Limit lawn areas. Since turfgrass, especially St. Augustine, can be the biggest water consumer in the yard, consider reducing the size of your lawn. There are many attractive drought-tolerant plant alternatives and handsome hardscape materials, such as light tan or gray gravel (white is too reflective and glaring).
- Choose low-water-use plants. Most plant growers and retailers tag their products to indicate water requirements. Nursery staff should be able to assist you in your selection.
- Water efficiently. Most low-water-use plants can do well with 1 inch of water per week. Be sure to group plants according to similar water requirements. Soaker hoses and drip irrigation systems are excellent means of delivering water directly to plants and reducing evaporation and runoff. They are particularly useful in vegetable gardens, in flower beds, and on slopes. Check your automatic sprinkler system periodically to ensure proper operation. If your system is programmable, you will probably want to use different settings for flower beds, vegetables, and lawns. Generally, lawns will require more frequent watering. If you use an end-of-hose sprinkler, choose one that delivers

large water drops close to the ground. Sprinkle early in the day to reduce water loss through evaporation.

- Practice good maintenance. Do not overfertilize, and weed as needed. Raise the lawn mower height in summer.

Remember that drought-tolerant plants, like others, require regular watering during the first year until they become established. Too often, thinking they are low-water-use plants, we water once or twice after planting and then are disappointed when the plants fail.

Mulch

While water conservation programs emphasize mulching to prevent loss of soil moisture, the benefits go far beyond. Here are five other good reasons to mulch:

1. To prevent soil compaction (a major problem with heavy clay soils) and erosion
2. To add organic matter and nutrients (if organic mulch is used) to soil as it breaks down
3. To moderate soil temperature
4. To suppress weeds
5. To prevent soil crusting in vegetable gardens

Many materials may be used as mulch: compost, wood chips, grass clippings, shredded bark, lava chips, pebbles, and decomposed granite.

Compost may need to be replenished more often than other materials, but it is my first choice, especially for vegetable and flower beds. It has good texture, does not pack down as some bark mulches do, and benefits the soil in so many ways. Some may prefer wood chips or shredded bark around trees and shrubs because they are

RECOMMENDED MULCH DEPTH (INCHES)

Flowers	Compost	1–2	Do not mulch flowers shorter than 3 inches.
	Shredded bark	1–2	Do not cover crown of plant.
Trees	Compost	1–3	Keep mulch 6 inches from trunk of tree.
Shrubs	Shredded bark	2–4	
Vegetables	Compost	3	Keep mulch 3 inches from plants.

longer lasting and neater looking. Decomposed granite is a great choice for succulents and cacti. Red lava and tumbled glass of a single or many colors can add a dramatic touch in special places, but it's difficult to maintain an unblemished appearance. They work best in small spaces where they won't get covered with leaves and other garden debris.

Grass clippings should be dried before being applied as a mulch. Green clippings will mold and mat down, becoming impervious to rain or overhead watering. Large wood chips look best used around trees and large shrubs.

 **FYI: Mulch**

Easy Gardening—Mulch (http://aggie-horticulture.tamu.edu/extension/easygardening/mulching/mulching1.html). Aggie Horticulture's site explains thoroughly and clearly in text and graphics how and why to mulch.

Irrigation Basics

I cringe when I think back to the long-ago days when I ran the overhead sprinkler all afternoon in the same spot. How much water was wasted running down the drive or evaporating before it ever hit the lawn I'll never know. Today I have less lawn to water, an underground sprinkler system programmed to go on at the crack of dawn, and a vegetable garden on a drip irrigation system. The landscape is an attractive mix of natives, adapted traditional landscape plants, and a few exotics for interest. And I use less water.

Water your lawn and plants only when they need it. Underwatered and overwatered plants show the same symptoms: leaves turn brown at the tips, go completely brown, and finally drop off.

- It is time to water the lawn if the grass lies flat or footprint impressions linger. Shrubs will droop; flowers will wilt. These clues are easy to read in summer, but it is just as important to water in winter if there has been little rain. Plants are dormant, not dead.
- Group plants of similar watering needs together.

- Water well both before and after applying mulch.
- Newly planted trees and shrubs need more frequent watering than established plants for one or two seasons.
- Just before or after dawn is an excellent time to water. Much water is lost to evaporation in the middle of the day; and nighttime watering can encourage fungus growth, especially in spring and fall when night temperatures fall.
- It's really easy to underwater when hand watering because the chore is so boring and the weather usually is very hot. When hand watering, be sure to water long enough to allow the water to penetrate the root zone to encourage deep root development.
- Consider a drip irrigation system for vegetable gardens and flower beds—even containers. Drip systems deliver water in a slow, controlled manner. Soil moisture and oxygen levels remain constant, soil temperature is moderated, and water is conserved because it is delivered where it is needed. As the price of water goes up and watering restrictions are imposed, drip irrigation can pay dividends.

TAKING CARE OF EQUIPMENT

- Check hoses. Washers on hoses wear out, and quick-connection parts become notorious leakers over time.
- Check underground sprinkler systems periodically. Wear and age also take their toll on them.
- Check drip emitters, which can clog.
- Check soaker hoses. These porous hoses age in the sun and spring leaks.
- Empty rain barrels monthly. If water is allowed to stand longer than two weeks, it may begin to smell. Add a capful of bleach to prevent smelly water and algae growth. Sediment can collect at the bottom of the barrel and interfere with water flow. Clean out the barrel completely at least once a year.

 **FYI: Water Use**

How Hot Weather Affects Plants from Texas A&M's Plant Answers (http://www.plantanswers.com/garden_column/june03/4.html) gives a clear explanation of just how and why hot weather is hard on our plants.

Texas Agricultural Extension Service's *Efficient Use of Water in the Garden and Landscape* is a superb, in-depth publication, explaining plants' use of water, watering methods, and responsible use of water resources (http://aggie-horticulture.tamu.edu/extension/homelandscape/water/water.html). It also contains an excellent discussion on drip irrigation.

CHAPTER 2

Gardening with Central Texas Soils

SOIL IS THE SKIN of the earth, a miraculous mixture of minerals, air, water, and organic matter—as old as the ages, ever changing. Ideally it is composed of 45 percent inorganic minerals, 5 percent organic matter, and 50 percent pore space shared equally by air and water. How well it performs in our gardens depends on its texture, structure, and chemistry.

Soil Texture and Structure

When we talk about clay, silt, loam, and sand, we are talking about soil texture—the size of the mineral particles of soil. In **clay** soils particles may be as small as .0001 inch, far too small to see. **Sand**, on the other hand, may be as large as .08 inch. **Silt** falls somewhere in between.

Equally important, the air space, or pores between the particles, also increases with the size of the particles. **Loam** is composed of all three particles. Sandy loam has more sand particles than silt or clay; clayey loam has more clay particles. Loam is said to be ideal mix for vegetables and many flowers. Unfortunately, that soil is very rare indeed in Central Texas. Soil structure refers to how the particles clump or hang together. Organic matter is important to soil structure; good soil structure is critical for nutrient and moisture retention and aeration.

Organic Matter

Much recent soil research has focused on the complexity of soil life and its influence on soil productivity. Soil life (from mammals and earthworms to insects,

COMPARISON OF SOIL CHARACTERISTICS

Clay	Sand
Slick and plasticlike to the touch when wet	Gritty to the touch
Warms up slowly	Warms up rapidly
Organic matter breaks down slowly	Organic matter breaks down rapidly
Cementlike when dry	Dusty when dry
Drains slowly	Drains quickly
High nutrient retention	Low nutrient retention

protozoa, algae, fungi, and bacteria) in the billions goes through its daily grind, living, eating, dying, and decomposing. Elements of soil life are constantly breaking down plant debris and one another and converting nutrients to usable forms. Channels are formed as all life moves through the soil. Soil particles are glued together by various secretions, forming large "crumbs." In the process of all this biotic activity nutrients are released and porosity, so critical for good drainage, is increased. Such soil is said to have good tilth.

Soil pH

The acidity or alkalinity of soil is measured on a pH scale from 0 (most acid) to 14 (most alkaline). A pH of 7 is considered neutral. When the pH is too high or too low, the ability of plants to use nutrients is reduced. The resulting deficiencies lead to poor growth and productivity. Although most things will grow in soil with a pH between 4 and 8, most flowers, fruits, and vegetables do best in soil with a pH between 6.5 and 7.0.

In many areas of Central and North-Central Texas, the soil is very alkaline, with a pH of 7.5 to 8.5 (the scale is geometric, not arithmetic, so an increase from a pH of 6 to a pH of 7 is a tenfold increase). At these levels iron is unavailable to plants, and many plants will suffer from iron chlorosis, a common but treatable problem. Symptoms of iron chlorosis are easy to identify: leaves yellow, but their veins remain green. Copperas, compost, sulfur, iron sulfate, or cottonseed meal can be added to the soil to help reduce its pH. Excessive acidity can be reduced quickly by adding lime, but this is not a common problem in Central Texas.

Soil pH should be checked before you embark on any major

planting. Also, find out the pH preference of the plants you wish to grow, and decide whether you want the extra trouble of maintaining the proper soil pH. If not, put those plants in containers or substitute with plants more tolerant of the native soil. Keep in mind that the water of much of the area is also alkaline.

Central Texas Soils

Texas Plants: A Checklist and Ecological Summary divides the state into ten vegetational regions (based upon climate, topography, plants, and soil types). Of these ten regions, four converge on Central Texas. Additionally, pockets of other vegetational regions occur in small areas. This is an important reason for getting a soil sample for your garden.

The eastern counties occupy the Blackland Prairies and the Post Oak Savannah. These fertile prairies are extensively cultivated. Blackland Prairie soils are largely calcareous (containing calcium) clay, although there are large sections of acid, sandy loams. This is the land farmers call ten o'clock dirt: at 9:55 A.M. it's too wet to plow, and at 10:05 A.M. it's too dry and hard; so you have to plow at 10:00. The Post Oak Savannah soils are acid and generally loamy.

To the north lie the Cross Timbers and Prairies, and the Edwards Plateau rises in the west. Basically, think of Interstate 35 as the dividing line between the Prairies and Savannah to the east and the Timbers and Plateau to the west. Some soils of the rolling north-central Cross Timbers contain a large portion of rock fragments. There the sandy to clay loams are neutral or slightly acid. The soils of the Edwards Plateau, or Hill Country, are mainly clay on top of limestone. They range from fairly deep in the eastern section to very shallow with a good percentage of rock fragments in areas west of the Balcones Escarpment.

Of course, one cannot leave a discussion of Central Texas soils without mentioning caliche. So common in the Hill Country, **caliche** is a light-colored layer of soil and gravel particles cemented together by calcium carbonate. Because it is difficult to penetrate, it limits root growth and nutrient retention and results in poor drainage and rapid runoff. Its high pH is inhospitable to many plants we wish to grow. It can be a few inches to several feet deep. Shallow caliche can be broken up with a pickax and discarded. If the caliche is too deep, consider another location or plant in a raised bed.

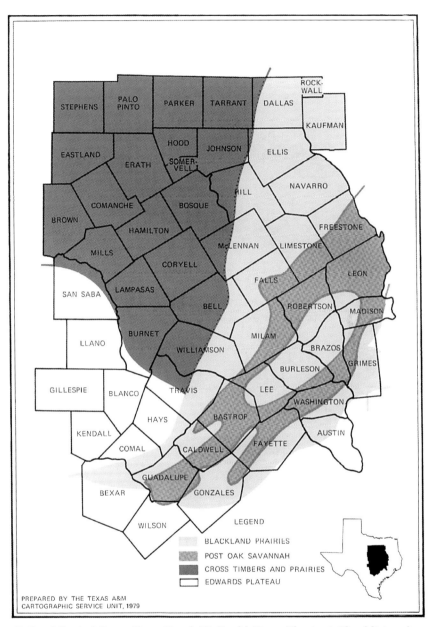

Soils of Central Texas (from Frank W. Gould, Texas Plants: A Checklist and Ecological Summary, *Texas Agricultural Experiment Station, 1975)*

Improving Soil

By now it's obvious that coping with our soil is a major key to successful gardening in Central Texas. What to do?

First, decide how you want to use the soil. Do you wish to plant flowers, trees and shrubs, and vegetables or install a lawn? This will determine how you go about improving the soil. Vegetables love loose, fertile soil, and many flowers share that preference. Trees and shrubs have extensive root systems that need to be encouraged to stretch out deeply and/or widely into the native soil. The selection of trees and shrubs that tolerate the properties of our native soils is essential. Whatever your soil type, incorporating a couple inches of organic matter before installing a new lawn is always welcome.

Second, get a soil test. This is probably the single most neglected garden chore. Yet by eliminating much of the guesswork, it can save you time, effort, and money. You can purchase a do-it-yourself kit, but its accuracy is highly dependent upon the skill and knowledge of the gardener. The preferred option is to take advantage of the comprehensive soil testing service available through Texas A&M University (http://soiltesting.tamu.edu/). For a nominal fee your soil will be tested for nitrogen, phosphorous, and potassium—the three primary elements in soil—and for trace elements and pH level. Along with the analysis you will receive recommendations for soil improvement according to its intended use. Allow about three or four weeks for results. Just before spring and fall planting seasons are the busiest times at the soil lab. The wait time will be shorter if you take your soil sample in the off season.

Improving Clay Soil for Flower and Vegetable Beds

Clay's major disadvantage is that it compacts so easily. When the air spaces are closed, water has no place to go and roots are deprived of air and nutrients. When the soil eventually dries out, it is as hard as a brick. Your goal is to open those spaces between the soil particles so soil life can nurture the plants:

1. Remove any rocks or stones.
2. Rototill or dig the soil to about one spade's depth, 8 or 9 inches, if possible. Repeated rototilling is no longer the popular garden practice

it once was. Among those who adhere to soil food web theory, rototilling is believed to damage soil structure and destroy much essential soil life. If you are starting from scratch in a compacted bed, however, it might be the first step to a new beginning.

3. Add 4 to 6 inches of organic matter. Rotted manure and mature compost are superb choices. Do *not* add sand to clay soil in hopes of improving drainage. You would have to replace 50 to 75 percent of the clay with sharp, gritty sand (not smooth, fine play sand) to succeed. Adding too little sand will only make your soil denser and create a cementlike substance, eliminating the desirable properties of clay.

4. If you are using a spade or fork, mix the additives by inserting the tool at an angle and turning it from side to side, rather than by inverting the soil. This turning method gives an even distribution by allowing the new material to filter down. The organic matter benefits soil by holding the fine clay particles together in large "crumbs" and by releasing nutrients as the matter decays. This

> ### WAYS TO AVOID COMPACTING CLAY SOIL
>
> 1. Never work clay soil when it is wet. You can undo all your good work in five minutes by tromping around and compacting the soil.
> 2. Use stepping stones if the area is to bear foot traffic.
> 3. Do not till excessively or overwork the soil. A healthy soil structure with adequate organic matter will maintain its tilth.

decomposition takes place rapidly at first, especially in our hot Texas summers, then slows considerably as the organic material becomes humus (an advanced state of decomposed organic matter). Since humus eventually breaks down into elements, organic matter must be added repeatedly to maintain good soil structure.

5. Allow the newly improved soil to settle for about a week before planting.

Soil Options

Sometimes improved native soil just isn't the right stuff. Container plants, exotics, and some vegetable seedlings are examples of plants that will do better in a different medium. Buying a prepared soil mix or even creating your own can mean the difference between a plant merely surviving and thriving.

Buying Soil

You may not have enough soil to improve, or you may not wish to spend the time and effort needed to develop a fertile, friable soil. You can always buy soil appropriate to your gardening needs. Build a raised bed (10 to 12 inches in height is ideal), and buy a soil mix to fill it. This is an excellent way to get off to a fast and easy, if more expensive, start.

Nowadays there are so many ways and places to buy soil. Dealers are offering more sophisticated blends, and customers know more about their needs. There are mixes for native plants, roses, vegetable gardens, or lawn topdressing. You can buy the bag, bag it yourself, or buy bulk (it certainly helps to have a pickup in this case).

Most blends are composed of a mineral base (often decomposed granite) enhanced by various composts and other organic matter. Buy from a dealer who has a good reputation, and ask the source of the soil blend. There are two things to avoid: "topsoil" unless it has been composted to destroy weed seeds; and the "sandy loam" used by contractors as a sod base at new homes. Often derisively referred to as "red death" for its orange-red color and lack of fertility, this soil is neither sand nor loam but a clay.

Unless you are buying small quantities, soil is sold by the cubic yard. To calculate your needs when planning or shopping, measure the area of the bed.

length (feet) x width (feet) × depth (feet) / 27 = number of cubic yards

Making Your Own Growing Medium

There are times when gardeners may need to make their own growing medium. Soil is needed for potted plants, for plants being "grown out" for planting in beds later, or for plants to be held over the winter in containers. There are all kinds of mixes available on the market, but one of the best recipes comes from the late

Doug Blachly, a renowned Austin gardener. His recipe meets all the criteria for soil: organic matter, fertility, and air space. It is simple and good:

2 parts compost or potting soil
1 part peat moss
1 part perlite

Plant Nutrients

Plants require sixteen nutrients. The three primary nutrients, which are needed in the greatest quantities, are nitrogen, phosphorus, and potassium.

Nitrogen stimulates growth and the production of plant protein and gives plants rich green color. It is especially important for leafy vegetables and large-leaved plants. However, it is an element that is quickly leached away. Plants that suffer from nitrogen deficiency may yellow, and their older leaves may drop. Stunted growth, delay in bud opening, smaller leaves, fewer flowers, and smaller fruit may also result from a lack of nitrogen. On the other hand, beware of the consequences of nitrogen oversupply: too-rapid growth that results in spindly, weak stems; too much leaf growth; and plants that bloom too late in the season, if at all.

Phosphorus stimulates vigorous growth of seedlings, the production of fibrous roots, and seed production. It is important in the production of plant sugars and for plants' efficient use of soil moisture. Plants deficient in phosphorus display symptoms similar to those of nitrogen deficiency. However, the leaves of phosphorus-deficient plants are usually dull green, tinged with purple. Often the entire plant is dwarfed. Symptoms of iron and zinc deficiencies may be evidence of excess phosphorus.

Potassium's role in plant nutrition is less easily defined than that of nitrogen and phosphorus. It is believed to contribute to normal cell growth through cell

division and to act as a catalyst in the formation of proteins, fat, and carbohydrates. Plants are heavy users of potassium, and a lack of it results in stunted plant growth and delay in plant development. Leaves may turn a purplish hue. Too much potassium may cause magnesium deficiency.

Calcium, magnesium, and sulfur are secondary nutrients generally supplied by soil. The eight remaining nutrients—iron, zinc, manganese, boron, molybdenum, copper, sodium, and chlorine—are trace elements. In our alkaline soils, iron and manganese are present but frequently inaccessible to plants.

Fertilizer

Even a casual reading of gardening literature quickly reveals a perplexing array of recommendations for fertilizing. This confusion is compounded when your nursery does not carry the particular formula you ask for but offers a substitute that you are not sure is comparable.

Making Sense of the Fertilizer Label
What do NPK, 8-2-4, and 20-20-20 mean? N (nitrogen), P (phosphorous), and K (potassium) are the symbols for the primary nutrients in fertilizer. They are stated on all fertilizer containers and always in that order. An 8-2-4 is a complete fertilizer, because it contains all three elements. The numbers signify the percentage of a given nutrient in the container: for example, a 100-pound bag of 8-2-4 fertilizer contains 8 pounds of nitrogen, 2 pounds of phosphorous, and 4 pounds of potassium. But wait, that doesn't add up to 100 pounds. What about the other 86 pounds? These are composed of fillers or "carriers" (they aid in distribution of the fertilizer). Sometimes they have nutrient value; sometimes they are inert. If a fertilizer has only one or two nutrients (20-0-0), it is considered incomplete. A balanced, complete fertilizer has all three nutrients in equal numbers (8-8-8).

Organic versus Inorganic
Before petrochemicals were introduced to agriculture and gardening, farmers and gardeners met their crops' and plants' nutrient needs with manure, cottonseed meal, bone meal, and blood meal. While many gardeners today insist that these organic sources are preferable to inorganics such as superphosphate, potassium chloride, and ammonium sulfate, it is difficult to find

ORGANIC

- Nutrients released slowly, especially in cold soil
- Comparatively expensive
- Little or no leaching or run-off
- Little or no threat of "burning" plants
- Improves soil structure
- Buffers pH
- Made from natural waste products, such as manures, seaweed, feathers, sewage sludge

INORGANIC

- Nutrients readily available for use, even in cold soil
- Inexpensive
- Can leach and run off into waterways
- No benefit to soil structure
- In excess, can result in plant "burn"
- Made from petrochemicals or natural gas processes

experimental evidence of differences in plants nourished by organic or inorganic nutrients. In general I prefer organic fertilizers because I believe they are more beneficial to soil life. In special cases, however, I am not hesitant to use a faster-acting inorganic product when needed.

Organic versus Inorganic Fertilizer

Fertilizers come in many forms. **Liquid** fertilizers are easy to store, deliver nutrients immediately, pose less risk of burning plants when diluted according to directions, and are good for container plants. They are usually applied more frequently than granular forms.

Granular products tend to be less expensive and easy to handle. They are excellent for fertilizing a large area such as a lawn or large vegetable garden.

Pelleted fertilizers are fertilizer balls coated with a permeable covering. The fertilizer is released over time with each watering. They are excellent for container plants. They are expensive but very convenient. Most last from three to four months.

Foliar feeding is valued for quickly delivering nutrients to plants. This method involves using water-soluble chemicals mixed with a prescribed amount of water and applying it directly to the entire plant with a watering can or sprayer. It is especially effective in situations in which obvious nutrient

Compost pile

deficiencies need correction. It is best to apply foliar fertilizer in the morning, when leaves absorb most efficiently, and when the temperature is 72°F or below. To prevent leaf burn, do not apply in full sun or allow droplets to form. Be sure to wet both sides of the foliage thoroughly. Because roots are the plant part designed for major uptake of nutrients, foliar feeding should not be considered a substitute method for delivering primary nutrients.

Whether you choose organic, inorganic, liquid, granular, or pelleted fertilizer, remember to always refer to the application recommendations on the label. So tempting to think one more scoop for good measure. Wrong! Too much fertilizer will result in "burning" (dehydrating) your plants. And because plants cannot use the extra fertilizer, it will be washed into the stream and river system during the next rain. If you apply too little fertilizer, your plants will fail to thrive.

Compost

Mix a pile of damp leaves, grass clippings, some vegetable wastes from the kitchen, and within several months you will be harvesting a crop of "black gold." The importance of organic matter to soil structure and chemistry has already been discussed. Compost is the least expensive and most readily available source of organic matter, or humus.

Making a compost pile just makes the gardener feel good, and it always produces, eventually. You get the satisfaction of cleaning up, recycling, and creating the best possible soil amendment. It can be as simple as a pile of leaves and grass clippings or as elaborate as a series of bins designated "new," "in progress," and "finished." Understanding the dynamic process of composting can prevent you from coming up with just another pile of soggy leaves at the end of the year.

Two types of bacteria—aerobic, which live in the presence of air, and anaerobic, which live in a wet, airless environment—decompose organic matter. Anaerobic bacteria tend to smell bad and work more slowly than aerobic bacteria. They are responsible for many people's fears about a "smelly" compost pile. Fortunately, they can be replaced by the aerobic variety by keeping the pile moist, not soggy, and by turning the compost to introduce oxygen, an element essential to the breakdown of the organic components. Confining composting materials in a bin (roughly 4 feet square and 4 feet high)

constructed of hardware cloth or wooden slats prevents compost ingredients from scattering and allows sufficient heat buildup. For convenience and appearance, compost bins, usually of black vinyl, are readily available at nurseries, garden centers, and hardware stores. The design and price range from simple and inexpensive to very sophisticated and pricey. They tend to keep things neat and, given the proper ratio of ingredients, cooking right along. They are excellent where space is limited.

Heat is generated by the multiplying organisms; its presence indicates that the compost pile is functioning. The optimum temperature range for a compost pile is 104°F to 140°F. Around 158°F the pile will suffer "thermal kill" and cool to somewhere within the optimal range. It's a delight on a nippy morning to see the steam rise when you wiggle an aerating stick in the middle of the bin and know that everything is going along just fine.

Moisture is another critical factor in the environment of bacteria. A healthy compost pile will be between 40 and 60 percent moisture, or as damp as a squeezed sponge. Below 40 percent, the rate of decomposition will decline; above 60 percent you risk having anaerobic bacteria, with their accompanying odors, take over. Using unchlorinated water from a rain barrel is a great way to keep those essential microbes churning.

Carbon and nitrogen present in organic matter provide the fuel and building materials for bacterial growth. Too little nitrogen will result in failure of the compost to heat up and a slow rate of decomposition. If the nitrogen level is too high, the compost pile may become too hot and beneficial microorganisms will be killed.

Ox or Elephant Beetle Grub

COMPOST INGREDIENTS
C (Carbonaceous)
Dry leaves
Hay, straw
Sawdust
Wood chips
Chopped cornstalks

BASICS FOR TIMELY
COMPOST
1. Carbon/nitrogen materials ratio of 3:1 by volume
2. Moisture—the damp sponge standard
3. Aeration—turn weekly
4. Sufficient size for heat retention—3 feet × 3 feet × 3 feet

N (Nitrogenous)
Vegetable kitchen waste (Be sure to bury it well into the pile to avoid attracting vermin and wildlife. After several undesirable encounters I have limited my own suburban compost pile to leaves and grass clippings)
Plant residues from *healthy* garden and grass clippings
Manures

You can see from the list that nitrogenous materials tend to be green, succulent, or leafy in comparison with woody, drier carbonaceous materials. If the compost seems to be working too slowly, you can add a little nitrogen in the form of fertilizer or some more grass clippings.

INGREDIENTS THAT SHOULD NOT BE INCLUDED

Chemically treated wood products. Sawdust from tree pruning is fine, but it is best not to use sawdust from construction sites. Wood used in construction can be chemically treated, sometimes with undesirable materials such as arsenic, copper, and chromium.

Poisonous plants such as poison ivy.

Diseased plants and weeds that have gone to seed. Your home compost pile may not reach the temperature of 140°F required to kill off seeds.

Animal products, including pet wastes and meat products. Meat wastes are very attractive to wildlife and neighborhood pets and are certain to spell trouble. Pet manures may carry organisms dangerous to people.

Grinding organic materials (particularly cornstalks and the woody parts of plants) is helpful but not necessary. It speeds the decomposition process. A variety of textures provides for air circulation and prevents compaction. Finished compost has a dark, rich color, an earthy smell, and a fluffy structure.

From time to time, we do see insects in the outermost layers of the pile, but they never appear in the finished product. Earthworms and grubs, on the other hand, are most welcome.

Chemical analyses show nitrogen levels of compost to be between 1 and 3 percent and phosphorous and potassium levels under 1 percent. For this reason, compost should never be considered a substitute for fertilizer. Instead, it should be used as a soil conditioner to increase water-holding capacity, provide air space and nutrients for soil microorganisms, and improve soil texture. Compost makes excellent mulch.

Compost Tea

In the last ten years compost tea has taken the gardening world, especially the organic world, by storm. Chicken soup for the garden! Recipes and brewing equipment advertisements on the Internet abound. And so do the controversial articles and opinion on its safety and efficacy. Essentially, compost tea is a mixture of water and compost that has been steeped and aerated for twelve to twenty-four hours, and to which additives such as molasses, yeast extract, and kelp have been added. These additives promote growth of the microbial mass. Compost tea must be applied to plants within eight hours of leaving the brewer or the microorganisms will die from lack of oxygen.

While compost tea is acknowledged as a weak fertilizer, hard evidence for claims that it works as a disease suppressant is lacking. There is also concern about human pathogens surviving the brewing process. In April 2004, the National Organic Standards Board released the Compost Tea Task Force Report with recommendations for the manufacture and use of compost tea. Organic gardeners largely believe the task force has erred on the side of caution; others disagree.

Renewing the soil is not a one-time chore—it needs to be done regularly. It's a living organism that needs your attention and care to remain healthy and the ideal environment for your plants.

 **FYI: SOIL**

Teaming with Microbes, a Gardener's Guide to the Soil Food Web by Jeff Lowenfels and Wayne Lewis (Timber Press, 2006). A clear and convincing discussion of how soil works, why it's important, and how we can help foster our soil life.

CHAPTER 3

The Gardener's Tools

Equipment

Equipment choices for the tool-happy gardener are almost endless (upgrades make wonderful gifts), but you can do a good job with a modest armory of tools. Following are the basics needed for garden and yard care.

Hoses. Measure the distance from your faucets to the farthest reaches of your yard, and buy the appropriate length of hose. A hose that is too short is frustrating, and one that is too long can drive you crazy with tangles and twists. Garden hoses are made of rubber, vinyl, or a combination of the two. Vinyl is lighter weight and cheaper. Rubber is heavy and tends to kink. A 5-ply hose of rubber/vinyl reinforced with tire cord fiber and with brass fittings is an excellent choice. Hoses will last longer if they are taken in during the winter months. Ultraviolet (UV) protection is also desirable in the Central Texas sun.

Should you want to avoid hauling hoses and sprayers from garden bed to garden bed without installing a full-fledged irrigation system, you can use porous **soaker hoses**. They drip or leak water at the ground level and, by delivering water directly to plant roots, are more efficient than sprayers. They also avoid

water loss from evaporation. Soaker hoses come in hard and soft versions, depending on the type of material used for construction. Take care of them like conventional garden hoses when a freeze is forecast.

Drip Soaker Tape. This is a flat tape with 1/2–1 gallon per hour (GPH) drippers pre-inserted every 12 inches. It is designed to be laid out aboveground to apply water directly to root zones of plants slowly and evenly. Its flexible design works well in most garden configurations. It is inexpensive and easy to work with.

Sprinklers and Nozzles. Hose-end lawn sprinklers come in a variety of shapes, sizes, patterns, and costs. What kind to use depends on the shape of your yard—square, rectangular, or irregular. Less water is lost to evaporation when it is delivered in heavy drops close to the ground. For all yard chores from watering flower beds to washing windows, nozzles with several settings work best. Rotate the head and go from gentle spray to sharp water jet, which is perfect for knocking pesky aphids from your plants.

Shovels. A **sharpshooter** has a long, slender, rounded shovel blade with a short handle. It is used for chopping, trenching,

moving small plants, and doing general-purpose work. A **round-point shovel** has a longer handle and a blade that is, as its name implies, rounded to a point. It is a great general-purpose shovel for clay soils. Remember that shovels are for digging, and they need to be sharp given our heavy soils. Periodically sharpen your shovel with a metal file. A friend keeps his shovels in a bucket of sand drizzled with linseed oil to keep them rust-free and sharp. Not a bad idea.

Forks. A four-tined fork is essential for turning soil. It is used for loosening, turning, and mixing soil and soil amendments. The fork is also handy for coaxing stubborn roots, but not large rocks, when transplanting small trees and shrubs.

Tamping Bar. Save your forks and shovels! The right tool for the right job was never more apropos. A 6-foot tamping bar is definitely the tool you want for digging out those large, often unexpected, rocks and roots.

Hoes. Hoes are indispensable for weeding, making planting rows, tamping soil, and doing other odd jobs. Some models have a curved metal piece, called a swan neck, from the end of the handle to the blade. This eases some of the chopping and digging action required to dig weeds or shape soil.

Rakes. A broad, plastic **leaf rake** is lightweight and excellent on lawns. For beds, an **adjustable-width rake** with metal tines is more convenient. A **garden rake** is a necessity for smoothing turned or tilled areas and for adjusting garden contours. Use the teeth to move soil and the back, or smooth, side to contour and level soil.

Mowers. There are two types of mowers (powered and manual) with two types of action (reel and rotary). The blades of a **reel mower** revolve against a cutting bar and cut the grass against it. A reel mower provides the most uniform cut and comes either gas powered or gardener powered. It is best for zoysiagrass. The blade of a **rotary mower** revolves on a horizontal plane. As the blade turns at high speeds, the sharp ends shear off the grass. Rotary mowers come in either gas-powered or electric-powered models and are best for buffalograss, St. Augustinegrass, and bermudagrass. A rotary blade dulls quite quickly under normal use and should be sharpened regularly (every six to eight weeks during the mowing season). Grinding wheels that fit on power drills are available at hardware and

garden stores. After sharpening, make sure that the blade is balanced so it won't damage the engine. Electric mowers are easy to start and less polluting than gas-powered mowers but are less powerful. If you are in the market for a new power mower, you will want one that bags *and* mulches.

Edgers. After mowing, edging is the finishing touch many people overlook, but one that makes the yard look trim and well kept. There are three choices in edgers. The first is a **manual edger**. This type of edger does not work well with our tough southern turfgrasses. The two other choices are either gas-powered or electric. They, in turn, come in two cutting types: blade or string. A **blade edger** has a metal blade that spins at high speed and trims grass evenly. This type works best along driveways, walks, and other hard-surface-to-grass areas. A **string edger** has a length of plastic line, or string, that spins at high speed to shear the grass. This can work along hard-surface-to-grass areas and can also be used with care around trees and other areas in the yard. Be sure to avoid slashing tree bark and shrub stems. Always wear protective eyeware when using edgers.

Saws. At least one good pruning saw is handy to have for removing dead and diseased limbs from trees and for shaping trees and bushes. If you leave most of the riskier work to professional tree trimmers, the saw you need can be small and compact.

Pruners. Shrubs, bushes, and small tree limbs will periodically need to be trimmed back. There are two types of pruners. The **anvil type** has a blade that comes down on a cutting bar. It is a good, sturdy tool for cutting dead twigs and branches but may crush living stems and limbs. The **pass-through type** is similar to scissors, with two cutting blades passing alongside each other. In general, I prefer the pass-through, or scissor, type because it cuts more cleanly. If you have larger limbs to cut, you can purchase a **lopper**, essentially a pruner with long handles to provide more leverage.

Hand Tools. When you work in a garden bed, two tools are essential: a trowel and a cultivator. The blade of a **trowel** looks like a small round-point shovel. Make sure you buy one that has a thin blade and a sharp edge. You will need these features to cut into garden soil. A **cultivator** is a three- or four-tined tool used to loosen soil and dig weeds.

Moving Equipment. In the garden you often find yourself moving heavy and large objects. Don't wait until your back goes out to acquire a mover—a **wheelbarrow** or **garden cart**. These are ideal for moving bulk items such as soil, compost, and mulch. But you should also consider including a **two-wheeled dolly**. Its flat, ground-level base plate allows you to slide it under pots or big rocks. This is one of those tools that makes you wonder why you didn't get it years ago. Nothing works better for hauling in tender potted plants when the forecast calls for frost or a freeze.

Big Bar of Soap. Many gardeners reject gloves for all but the toughest jobs. Gloves may protect and keep your hands clean, but when planting six packs of vegetables and 4-inch pots of flowers, you need to feel your way around, know how those plants are set in the soil, and manipulate the roots. To prevent hard-to-remove soil from getting under your fingernails, rake your nails across a bar of soap and leave the soap under your nails. When it is time to clean up, just remove the soap with a small nail brush. No more multiple scrubbings to remove the efforts of a day in the garden.

This inventory will get you through many gardening seasons.

But if you are like most gardeners, you will soon want more. Before long you will find yourself drifting toward the garden tool display and thinking that "if only I had that flat-bladed shovel, I could . . ."

Resources

Books, fact sheets, Web sites, videos, blogs, and in-store classes. The list of resources for the gardener or home owner is long and growing—a welcome but sometimes dizzying change from the days when information was limited to a single gardening bible.

The following resource lists are composed of books, other print materials, and Internet Web sites I use frequently. They reflect personal gardening interests as well as confidence in the quality of information.

Books

Sam Cotner, *The Vegetable Book* (Waco: TG Press, 1985). This is *the* complete guide to vegetable gardening in Texas. A chapter is devoted to each of the vegetables we grow in the state.

Howard Garrett, *The Dirt Doctor's Guide to Organic Gardening* (Austin: University of Texas Press, 1995). This book is fun and immensely informative; Garrett's enthusiasm, wit, and style will lead many a reader down the organic garden path.

Stephen W. Kress, *The National Audubon Society: The Bird Garden* (London: Dorling Kindersley, 1995). An ornithological writer tells how to select vegetation that will attract birds. In this beautiful volume you will learn what birds are attracted to specific plants and how to plan for food, water, and shelter needs as well as nesting sites. The entire country is covered region by region.

Native and Adapted Landscape Plants, 4th ed. (Austin: City of Austin and Texas Cooperative Extension, 2005). A basic, comprehensive, no-frills catalog of plants for Central Texas. Water conservation, pest and deer resistance, and low maintenance are weighed heavily in the selections.

Scott Ogden, *Garden Bulbs for the South* (Dallas: Taylor Publishing, 1994). If you want to grow bulbs in Central Texas, this book is a must. Find out why you have never had luck in our area with many traditional spring-blooming bulbs and learn about alternatives.

Scott Ogden, *Gardening Success with Difficult Soils* (Dallas: Taylor Publishing, 1992). This book is a valuable tool for gardeners selecting plants for and working in limestone and alkaline clay soils.

Elizabeth Stell, *Secrets to Great Soils* (Pownall, VT: Storey Communications, 1998). Concise and immensely readable, this paperback book informs without being academic. How to create fertile soil, the benefits of mulch and compost, and soil-working tools are lucidly covered.

Sunset Western Garden Problem Solver (Menlo Park, CA: Sunset Books, 1998). Although the excellent Sunset garden books are tailored more to the western states, they have much information to share with us. The *Problem Solver* is a virtual encyclopedia of all troubles in the garden, from bugs, weeds, diseases, and soil problems to what construction can damage. Well organized and copiously illustrated, there is no more comprehensive resource.

Sally Wasowski with Andy Wasowski, *Native Texas Plants, Landscaping Region by Region* (Houston: Gulf Publishing, 1991). An extensive guide to native flowers, trees, shrubs, and ground covers, this handsome volume is extremely helpful to those who might wish to learn about Texas flora as well as those who garden.

The Wasowskis' newer *Native Texas Gardens* (Houston: Gulf Publishing, 1997) is equally authoritative and attractive.

William C. Welch, *Perennial Garden Color* (Dallas: Taylor Publishing, 1989). This book is a comprehensive review of perennials that grow well in the South, including Central Texas. The explanations are direct and informative, and most of the photographs (and there is at least one for each plant listed) will provide the gardener with an idea of how the plant will look when grown and in bloom.

Doug Welsh, *Texas Garden Almanac* (College Station: Texas A&M University Press, 2007). Written by the Texas statewide coordinator for the Texas Master Gardener program who is also a professor at Texas A&M University, this authorative book covers all of gardening and is organized around the calendar year. It is comprehensive, inviting, and charmingly illustrated.

Magazines
A growing trend in garden magazines is to refer readers at the end of articles to videos on their Web sites. This is an excellent way to make pruning, planting, and other garden procedures perfectly clear.

Texas Gardener (P.O. Box 9005, Waco, TX 76714) is a bimonthly magazine with articles that tend toward propagation and vegetable gardening, although there are articles on annuals and perennials that do well in Texas. It contains excellent month-by-month information on gardening activities (www.texasgardener .com).

Neil Sperry's Gardens (400 W. Louisiana, McKinney, TX 75069) is published bimonthly. This magazine focuses on landscape design and shrubs, trees, and flowers (www.neilsperry.com).

Fact Sheets
The **Agricultural Extension Service at Texas A&M University** produces some of the highest-quality gardening literature anywhere—and most of it is free. Drop by your local County Extension Office and check the pamphlets in their inventory. You will find short articles on a wide variety of topics. If the county horticultural extension agent or a volunteer Master Gardener is around, you can probably get some free advice as well.

Grow Green Fact Sheets on many garden topics are produced jointly by the City of Austin and Texas Cooperative Extension and are available free at area garden centers.

Internet

The Internet has put the entire plant world at our fingertips. What a boon to gardeners— obscure facts about every plant and gardening practice just a click away. Web sites of distant growers have introduced us to plants never found at our local nurseries. In a flash we have gone from too little information to far more than we can cope with. Information management has replaced information scarcity. Bookmark lists grow out of control, and Web sites come and go, are updated infrequently, or simply abandoned. Superb information is available at university-supported agricultural extension sites, government agencies, and commercial sites. Many local nurseries have Web sites that not only advertise specials but also offer calendars of local garden events and excellent plant and gardening information. Blogs and forums allow gardeners to share real-life gardening experiences, which are often the best. But beware, quality varies—widely. As

technology improves, sites get better all the time. Videos of gardening how-tos are now common offerings. More topic-specific sites appear in the FYI sections throughout this book.

Aggie Horticulture (http:// aggie-horticulture.tamu.edu) is the go-to-first Web site for Texas gardeners. Maintained by the Horticulture Department at Texas A&M University, it has information on all aspects of gardening and agriculture for Texas. Because of its size, climate, number of vegetation zones, and varied soils, Texas presents special challenges to the gardener. So much of the information we need to succeed in our gardens is specific to our location. And here it is— from planting dates, appropriate plant varieties, to soil care and irrigation practices. To find your county extension agent, click on "County/Regional" and then "County Extension Offices."

The Arizona Master Gardener Manual (http://ag.arizona.edu/ pubs/garden/mg/) is wide ranging and well organized. Selection of topics covered includes basic botany, plant pathology, vegetable gardening, pesticide use and safety, and water quality and use (they should know!). Available online, or you can order a hard copy from the Web site.

Central Texas Horticulture (http://aggie-horticulture.tamu .edu/travis/) has gardening information, publications, news, and community events from the Texas AgriLife Extension Service Office in Travis County. When it comes to gardening, local is good.

Dave's Garden (http://daves garden.com/) is a gardening universe. Don't lose yourself in this Web site and forget to get to work in the garden. Favorite sections are the databases in Plantfiles, a collaborative effort of contributions by thousands of gardeners, and Garden Watchdog, which rates gardening mail-order companies for quality, price, and service.

Extension Earth-Kind (http:// earthkind.tamu.edu/) from Texas A&M University uses research-proven techniques to provide maximum gardening and land-scape enjoyment while preserving and protecting our environment. Providing expert information on everything from home landscaping, pest management, water conservation, and roses, it is a treasure.

Grow Green (http://www .ci.austin.tx.us/growgreen/) is a partnership effort by the City of Austin and the Texas Cooperative Extension. This site provides a wealth of information on gardening in Central Texas, selecting native and adapted plants, using water wisely, and maintaining and adapting the garden to the needs of the environment.

The Gardening Launchpad (http://gardeninglaunchpad.com/ Aus.html) has been maintained for years by Jim Parra, retired garden center coordinator of Austin's Zilker Botanical Garden. Information about weather, plants, problems, area events, organizations, garden clubs, and excellent hyperlinks to gardening resources are just part of Jim's generous offering.

A Green Guide to Yard Care (http://www.tceq.state.tx.us/ comm_exec/forms_pubs/pubs/ gi/gi-028.html) offers a concise and to-the-point PDF file on landscape design and yard care, including air-pollution prevention to Integrated Pest Management. Its composting information is excellent.

Missouri Botanical Garden's Kemper Center for Home Gardening (http://www.mobot.org/gardeninghelp/plantinfo.shtml) is a superb Web site. Take your time to explore its well-presented and organized abundant plant and gardening information.

National Gardening Association (http://www.garden.org/home) is a handsome site full of all kinds of gardening information, including nicely done how-to videos on a variety of topics, such as creating a container garden, dividing perennials, and making raised beds.

Texas AgriLife Extension Bookstore (https://agrilifebookstore .org/) puts all AgriLife Extension publications on topics from lawn and garden, animals, water conservation, and government to disaster preparedness in your hands or on your screen. You can purchase hard copies of publications or download for free. From the site you can e-mail questions to Extension experts. Take advantage of this superb resource.

Texas Parks and Wildlife's Texas Wildscapes Nongame and Urban Program (http://www.tpwd. state.tx.us/huntwild/wild/wildscapes/) offers information and even a certification program in gardening for wildlife. The mail-

ing address is TPWD, 4200 Smith School Road, Austin, TX 78744.

Forums and Blogs
These are great sites for information and inspiration. Be careful, they can become addictive.

Blotanical (http://www.blotanical.com/) is a global gardening blog directory. Here you can search for blogs by geographical location, content, or bloggers' names. Click on a location on the map or search by keyword. The number of Central Texas blogs is astounding. The site is very well done and a total treat.

GardenWeb (http://forums.gar denweb.com/forums/txgard/) will connect you with Texas plant exchanges and conversations.

Garden Clubs
Garden clubs are treasure troves of gardening information, general or plant specific, and they are a good way to meet real gardeners who have lots of experience gardening in the community. Your county extension agent can help you locate a garden club in your area. Check your government blue pages for the telephone number of your agent, or on the Web, go to http:// texasextension.tamu.edu/.

CHAPTER 4

Creating a Garden— Designing a Landscape

OVER THE MANY years I have gardened in Central Texas, I have embraced, or been influenced by, almost every trend and gardening ideology from Martha Stewart Perfect, to Xeriscape, color theme, organic, native plants only, and gardening for wildlife. I have had some nice successes and some abysmal failures. My garden is my science lab, art studio, sanctuary, and place of meditation. It is defined as much by what crawls, hops, hovers, slithers, and flies in and through it as by what grows in it. And although I resolve every year to concentrate on design, it hasn't happened yet. An intense love for plants and a need to try them all (greedy gardeners are a numerous lot) derail my best intentions. The needs of my plants design much of my garden. It is not a conventionally beautiful garden, but it is endlessly fascinating. There is one small spot where I can stand still for ten minutes and not take in everything growing, happening in that wee space before my eyes. The garden changes all the time. It changes color as flowers bloom and fade. It changes shape as some plants grow tall and others go dormant and disappear. It changes mood as the light brightens or dims. It is ever a wonder; it is never finished. It is the embodiment of my favorite gardening quote:

> As long as one has a garden one has a future, and as long as one has a future one is alive.

> *Frances Hodgson Burnett, author of* The Secret Garden

When I think of a home landscape, I see a scene with a large structure (a house) in it. I see shapes, lines, spaces, colors, and textures. I look for coherence, balance, contrast, and a theme. I think, "What do I want to do here? Where do I want to lead the eye? Do I want to create a sense of distance or perhaps define a shape?" Here I am using plants (and other materials) to implement a design, an intention. Whether one begins with a plan or with plants, order must be established and maintained. There needs to be a reason for what we do.

For years I considered the design principle of "sense of place" sacrosanct. Certainly the powerful beauty and character of the Hill Country are gifts to Central Texas worthy of preserving in our own landscapes. But "sense of place" may be less compelling, or even difficult to define, if you live in a subdivision (geometric lots defined by privacy fences) that was until recently a cotton field or cornfield. Lately Central Texas has taken on a tropical look that was unimaginable even ten years ago. Palms are everywhere, and the tropical bird of paradise (*Caesalpinia pulcherrima*) and firebush (*Hamelia patens*) brighten our landscapes from late spring through fall with their vibrant colors. Garden design today is free and open to innovation, like our architecture, and not tethered to the prescriptive or constricting traditional.

We have more plants and products—more and better designers. Hardscape has gone from a utilitarian feature to a major design element, reducing water needs as well as visually enriching the landscape.

Many Central Texas urban and suburban landscapes are nothing less than exhilarating and dramatic. You can get excellent ideas during neighborhood drives or, better yet, walks. Neighborhoods that are being updated are especially ripe for good design ideas. Newer high-end malls and commercial developments can be great places to see stunning plant combinations that thrive under challenging conditions like harsh all-day sun and reflective surfaces. Area garden tours, a favorite, give access to imagination and an array of styles and plant materials in a local setting—much superior to glossy magazine layouts of distant locales. After years of attending these tours, I find I enjoy best those gardens that are loved and have originality and surprise.

Really Basic (s)

Whether you are creating a garden or designing a setting for your home, doing it yourself or hiring a designer, the more thought you give to the following essential considerations, the easier the process will be. A plan on paper is a good place to start. Drawn to scale is even better. It will help you calculate the number of plants and other materials you will need and show current spaces and areas shaded by existing trees. Sometimes we bring our inside thinking to the outdoors and fail to realize that outdoor scale is much larger than that indoors. Making beds and paths too small and pinched looking is a common but easily avoidable mistake. Also, when making your plan, keep in mind the plan on paper views the site from overhead, but you will experience it from ground level and from many angles as you move about.

- Use—How will the space be used? Family needs, children and pet activities?
- Existing plants—Are they doing well? Why or why not? Too much shade or neglect? How can they be used in the new plan? Will they restrict, or can they be useful?
- Soil—What is your soil like? Consider its texture, moisture-holding capacity, pH, and depth.
- Sunlight—How much is necessary, and what kind?

All day or half day, morning or afternoon, filtered or full?

- Water conservation—Incorporate good water-saving practices in all parts of your plan (see "Water Conservation—a Part of Every Landscape and Garden Plan" in chapter 1).
- Easements and boundaries—You may need to keep an open space for access for utility companies; you will definitely want to avoid conflicts with neighbors.
- Utility location—You need to plan around AC units, water faucets, points of egress, and sprinkler heads.
- Impact on whole scene—Often we see our gardens, yards, and landscapes too narrowly. We may notice a bare place and fill it without considering how it will fit with the shape, texture, and color of other elements. Consider also the views from inside the house.
- Time—What will the new scheme look like in each season? Or five years? And finally, your own time. Does the new plan demand more time spent on attention and maintenance than you care to give? Is it too complicated?

Selecting the Right Plants for Central Texas

The plants listed in the following chapters were selected by several criteria: some plants are too useful and successful in Central Texas to ignore; some are old-fashioned workhorses that I rejected at one time, only to appreciate later their desirable attributes; others are sentimental favorites; and some reflect newer fashions. I have also included some plants that I have grown successfully, enjoyed enormously, and think should be used more in Central Texas.

Two favorites, azaleas and gardenias, have been omitted. Always a labor of love in much of Central Texas, their need for acid soil and plenty of water makes them inappropriate choices for our environment. A well-established gardenia can make it through the summer on a mandatory twice-a-week watering schedule, but that is a real challenge for the shallow-rooted azaleas. However, they both do well in pots, which is an option for devoted admirers.

Following are four Web sites to help you take that first step to successful gardening.

Texas Superstars (http://www .texassuperstar.com/). The  Coordinated Education and Marketing Assistance Program (CEMAP) is an industry–Texas A&M University cooperative program that identifies landscape plants with the potential to thrive in large areas of Texas. Potential candidates undergo trials and, if selected (ability of the plant to be mass produced is one criterion), go into production. They are then promoted and marketed. The CEMAP program's purposes are to "provide highly effective marketing assistance to growers and retailers, particularly during slower periods of the nursery year" and to "ensure that consumers utilize the very best and most environmentally responsible plant materials, products, and horticultural techniques."

Texas Superstars include annuals, perennials, woody shrubs, trees, water lilies, and even a tomato. The Web site includes growing tips and information on how Superstars are selected. These plants are well vetted, so if you are new to Central Texas or to gardening or just tired of having your plants die, this is a great place to start.

Earth Kind Plant Selector (http://earthkind.tamu .edu/EKSelector.html). This excellent site allows you to search by region or zip code for plants that are numerically rated for heat, drought and pest tolerance, as well as soil and fertility requirements. The Web site has a link to a list of Texas invasive plants, which gives recommendations for appropriate substitute plants.

Plants for Texas (http://www. plantsfortexas.com/). Through its Plants for Texas program, nursery wholesaler Magnolia Gardens offers a growing list of native and nonnative plants that have been tested and proven to be successful in Central Texas and beyond. The Web site includes a list of retailers and links to cultural requirements for all listed plants.

Sustainable Urban Landscape Information Series (http:// www.sustland.umn.edu/).

This well-designed site from the University of Minnesota promotes good design principles with environmentally sound, functional, and sustainable landscaping methods. Its discussion of color in the landscape is lucid and sophisticated.

Central Texas Plants for Dry Shade

Finding plants that thrive in dry, shady conditions is one of gardening's more trying quests, and finding flowering plants for those situations is even more difficult. I have read many lists, and frankly, I suspect a bit of padding. The problem is that *shady* and *dry* are rarely defined precisely. The following plants have done well in my garden with supplemental watering once every two weeks and in total shade for at least two-thirds of the day and/ or heavily filtered sun all day. Add compost before planting to increase the soil's capacity to retain moisture, and remember that all plants need to receive regular watering to become established. The more dense the shade, the less profuse the flowers and less lush the foliage are likely to be.

Ground Covers and Accents

Algerian Ivy does well in heat and heavy shade. It is a very tough plant and less invasive than English ivy.

Aspidistra, including the dwarf variety, 'Milky Way,' is the *most* dry shade–tolerant plant. It does well in moist soil, too, but cannot tolerate sun. Aspidistra is one of the very few plants that can survive total shade.

Holly Fern prefers moisture but can acclimate to dry conditions once it is well established.

Inland Sea Oats prefers moisture but can acclimate to dry conditions once it is well established.

Liriope, including the giant variety, presents handsome strap-leaved foliage for textural variety.

Twistleaf Yucca gives a nice southwestern look under the heavy shade of live oaks and other trees.

Perennials

Brazilian Sage does nicely with average watering. It will bloom more generously with a bit more sun but acclimates easily to less.

Cedar Sage is the nice little bright red sage seen at the base of Ashe junipers (a harsher place to grow is hard to imagine) in the woods. It has lovely, vivid red flowers in spring and attractive gray-green fuzzy foliage most of the year.

Purple Heart is a hard one to kill. Sun or shade, it keeps putting out trailing purple leaves and pinkish flowers spring to fall.

Shrubs

Aucuba or Gold Dust Plant will tolerate dry soil well but is easily sunburned.

Chile Pequin is small leaved and delicate but will produce peppers in a fair amount of shade.

Dwarf Chinese Holly is tough and versatile and looks good everywhere.

Japanese Yew has long, needlelike leaves and a handsome columnar shape, adding texture and line to the landscape.

Nandina thrives just about anywhere.

Sandankwa Viburnum is an outstanding evergreen shrub with one of the most stunning shades of green.

Turk's Cap will wilt when parched, but it hangs in there. Its spiraled flowers are charming and beloved by hummingbirds. Like many tough plants, it is persistent. Consider its location carefully.

Yaupon, multitrunked or dwarf, is very tolerant of widely varying conditions.

Butterflies

Thanks to educational efforts by conservation organizations, many gardeners realize the richness other living creatures bring to their world. The first year of my butterfly garden, it was easy to forget about the plants because there was so much to do—observing and identifying everything that flew in. And in they flew. Of the more than 160 butterfly species recorded in Travis County, I had counted 70 in my roughly 1,000-square-foot garden. First came the butterflies to nectar from the flowers. Next, eggs were deposited, singly or in masses, on the undersides of leaves, then the telltale chewed leaves, and finally the chrysalises, some in very unexpected places.

The emergence of a butterfly from a chrysalis is a thrilling event—such a magnificent transformation in a time of total vulnerability. The process takes time and usually happens in early morning. Fluid courses through the veins of the butterfly's wings to make them unfurl. Then the body and wings have to set before the butterfly can fly away. There, immobile and defenseless, the butterfly hangs before the world. Usually we glance at

Giant swallowtails mating

Pipevine swallowtail chrysalis

Black swallowtail larva

Pipevine swallowtail caterpillar morphing from larva to chrysalis

Gulf fritillary

butterflies for only a moment or two as they flit by, but by observing a butterfly at length, we can follow from its emergence— fresh, brilliant, and color saturated—through its last ragged and faded days. It has mated and done its job, but that last moment is always a little sad. The life span of butterflies (excluding egg, larva, and chrysalis stages) varies by species. Monarchs can live to nine months, but the majority of butterflies live about two to four weeks.

Quickly, the butterfly garden gets quite complex, or has been but has not been noticed. Joining the butterflies are paper wasps, always cruising near ground level looking for caterpillars, and other predator insects. Aphids attack the milkweeds, and ladybugs come after the aphids. Hummingbirds arrive to nectar on the flowers, snatching lurking crab spiders, if lucky; lesser goldfinches perch on seedheads of coneflowers and cosmos. Anoles and skinks thrive, and Carolina wrens love it all. But it is not the peaceable kingdom the gentle name "butterfly garden" implies. Violent and dramatic things happen. Species populations fluctuate wildly. Some return; some do not—at least in the short term. Of all the gardens I have had, the butterfly garden is the most riveting and engaging. The magnifying glass and binoculars join the

Pipevine swallowtail larvae devouring white-veined pipevine

Red admiral nectaring

trowel and pruners in the garden tool kit. And the garden is redefined.

BUTTERFLY GARDEN BASICS
- Nectar plants for adult butterflies—Butterflies are attracted to many flowers, native and adapted.
- Larval food plants for caterpillars—Although I have suffered few outright losses to caterpillar damage, it is best to consider these plants as dispensable.
- Water—Water used for plants in the garden is sufficient, but butterflies also like wet, muddy spots to puddle in. This is how they get their minerals.
- Sun—Both butterflies and the plants that support them like sun. Butterfly activity is less on cloudy and windy days.
- Close-focus binoculars—For observing butterflies, you will want binoculars that focus down to 3 or 5 feet. They are essential for butterfly identification.
- Pesticides should never be used in a butterfly garden.

Best Butterfly Plants for Most Common Butterfly Species

To fully enjoy and appreciate the many pleasures of the butterfly garden, you will want to provide food sources for both the larval and adult stages of the butterfly. Expect your larval plants to be well chewed, even to disappear completely. The nectar of flowers that support the adults is frequently shared with hummingbirds, bees, and other insects.

Larval Food Plants
Common hackberry—Mourning cloak, question mark, snout, tawny emperor. The bane of many gardeners and home owners, the common hackberry provides food and shelter for a large variety of butterflies and birds.

Dill—Eastern black swallowtail

Dutchman's pipe (*Aristolochia tomentosa*) and white-veined Dutchman's pipe (*A. fimbriata*)—Pipevine swallowtail. *A. tomentosa* is a Texas native; *A. fimbriata* is a native to South America but thrives here and is an exceptionally beautiful low-growing vine. After being eaten back to the ground by caterpillars, it will recuperate in time to feed the next brood.

Fennel—Eastern black swallowtail

Lantana—Painted lady

Milkweeds—Monarchs and queens

Oaks—Live, bur, and chinquapin oaks attract a variety of hairstreaks and duskywings.

Parsley—Eastern black swallowtail

Passionflower (native and adapted varieties)—Gulf fritillary and zebra longwings

Nectar Plants

Bonesets and several species of blue mist flowers—Queens and hairstreaks

Milkweeds—Monarchs and queens like all milkweeds, but tropical milkweed (*Asclepias curassavica*) has been the easiest to grow in the garden and attracts the largest number of butterflies. Expect aphids, too.

Pentas—Many species are attracted to pentas.

Sennas—Sulphurs and sennas just go together.

Summer phlox—Swallowtails

Texas thistle—Painted lady, swallowtails, and others

Verbena—Many butterflies like members of the verbena family. Tall verbena (*Verbena bonariensis*) is a favorite of many butterfly species, bees, and hummingbirds.

Zinnias—Many species. Simple, old-fashioned varieties seem to attract the most butterflies.

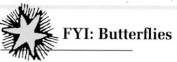

FYI: Butterflies

Butterflies of Texas (http://www.utexas.edu/tmm/tnhc/entomology/butterfly/index.html). Butterfly facts, checklists, and discussion of butterfly gardening in Central Texas by Texas Memorial Museum, University of Texas at Austin.

Travis County Butterfly Checklist (http://www.texasento.net/Travislist.htm). Included in the checklist is a good month-to-month calendar of species-occurrence data. Data are valid for much of Central Texas.

Native Plants

Central Texas is fortunate to have a rich and large collection of native flora and fauna. The arguments for using these native plants in our home landscapes are strong and grow more convincing each year: increased biodiversity, water conservation, wildlife support, and natural heritage preservation. As I have gradually but increasingly replaced many "garden varieties" in my garden and landscape with native plants, I have reaped many rewards and have had some interesting revelations. Certainly the increased biodiversity that has resulted from the creation of a butterfly garden has added immeasurably to the interest and condition of the garden. I no longer use pesticides of any kind—no longer need them. This is due in part to a shift toward greater tolerance of chewed, sometimes devoured, plants and a healthier garden (bugs do eat bugs). I also get more interesting birds stopping by during the spring and fall migrations; the residents have a good food source for their young. I like the seasonal variations and dynamics.

However, early experiences with native plants were not without disappointment. I did not anticipate that the feel and character of a landscape based solely on native plants would be so distinctly different from the traditional one I was replacing. Some of the shrubs and understory trees are scruffy and shapeless; some enchanting, but small flowers drop out of view unless planted in masses. It is quite different from planting broad-leaved evergreens whose full and lush year-round appearance is predictable, or a packet of zinnias or a flat of pentas that will bloom their hearts out all summer. Native plants have adapted to heat and drought in many ways—small leaves or a short blooming season followed by a long dormant period. These characteristics may not be consistent with the home owner's intentions. Some native shrubs, such as kidneywood and yaupon, can be spindly in the field but respond very well to shaping by pruning. The Texas mountain laurel, on the other hand, should never be trimmed severely. Removing too much growth at one time eventually may cause the plant to die. The use of the exquisite Texas sage as a hedge plant and subjecting it to regular geometric trimming is a sad, but common, misuse.

Many who believe that a native plant is bound to work just because it is a native, particularly if labeled a Central Texas native, are surprised to learn that native plants can occupy a narrower optimal range of soil, moisture, and light than many horticulture cultivars that have been bred for their wide tolerances. Know your plants and site, and with appropriate expectations, designing with native plants is an exciting adventure, not a failed experiment.

We Central Texans are fortunate to have an abundance of information resources and commercial providers of native plants:

Lady Bird Johnson Wildflower Center (http://www.wildflower.org/). Its printed materials, Web site, and many outstanding classes and programs throughout the year offer unrivaled information on native plants. Go to "Explore Plants" on the menu for a terrific plant database, photo gallery, checklist of recommended natives for Central Texas, and list of suppliers and organizations. This site has it all. Twice a year (spring and fall), the center holds native plant sales of unsurpassed selection. They are not to be missed by anyone interested in using native plants or just wanting to see and learn about them.

Native Plant Society of Texas (http://npsot.org/wp/). A member-based organization with chapters throughout the state, NPSOT promotes conservation, use of native plants, and education. Local chapters sometimes participate in plant sales.

Texas Plant Information (http://www.texasento.net/plnts.htm). A huge site with excellent links to butterfly gardening, bee gardening, taxonomy, native plant identification, databases, organizations, weeds, and deer-resistant plants.

Ponds and Water Gardens

Nothing transforms the landscape like a water garden. A water garden creates a new

Water lily

Aquatic canna

environment, producing, in turn, a new realm of possibilities and interests—new plants, new fauna, new garden experiences. Submersible pumps, low-cost molded fiberglass or plastic pools, and easy-to-work-with PVC liners have made ponds affordable and possible for every home landscape. Ponds, however, are a commitment and really do require careful planning and regular maintenance—talk to those who have ponds as well as experts when doing your research. Before you dig, consider these elements:

Location. Even the simplest ponds take more than a bit of work to install, so think hard

Red neon dragonfly on equisetum

about location. Do you want the pond to be visible from the house? If you want water lilies, you will need at least five hours of sun. You will need access to a water hose and probably an electrical outlet. The pond will need to be level. Deciduous trees directly overhead will drop their leaves, which may be harmful to aquatic life and clog filters and pumps.

Materials. If you use a PVC liner, it should be 20–40 mils thick. Molded plastic pools should come with a five- to ten-year warranty. Tubs, barrels, and water troughs make great simple aboveground water gardens. Although it is not absolutely necessary, you will most likely want a pump and filtration system to keep water circulating and trap debris. Be sure to get one appropriate for the size of your pond.

Maintenance. Getting the pond in balance to support aquatic life may take some time. Chemicals may be necessary to control pH and other factors. Filters need to be cleaned weekly to keep them functioning properly; ponds need to be cleaned of debris periodically. Circulating water and Mosquito Dunks will help control mosquitoes.

Plants for Ponds and Bogs

Deep-water plants require lots of sun, still water, and regular fertilizer. Water lilies, both tropical water lilies and hardy varieties, and aquatic cannas are the stars of the deep-water plants.

Bog or marginal plants grow in mud at the edge of ponds or in water ½ to 6 inches deep. Bog plants include iris, horsetails, rushes, and sedges. These plants provide good habitat for aquatic wildlife.

Submerged plants add oxygen to the water garden during the day and at night absorb carbon dioxide. They compete with algae by removing unwanted and excess nutrients from the water. American pondweed, waterstargrass, elodea, and parrotfeather are good examples of submerged plants.

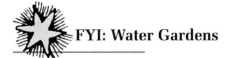 **FYI: Water Gardens**

Water Gardeners International (http://www.watergardeners international.org/clubs/main.html) is an international directory of water garden clubs, societies, and organizations. The site is a marvel and an adventure. There

are more than a dozen listings for Texas. Pond society members are as an enthusiastic a group as I have ever seen; they are always eager to enlist or assist anyone interested in ponds.

Water Gardens—A Low Management Approach, Oklahoma State University Cooperative Extension Service (http://pods.dasnr .okstate.edu/docushare/dsweb/ Get/Document-3588/NREM-100web%20color.pdf) provides straightforward and clear information, including a nice explanation of how a water garden ecosystem works.

Container Gardens

Everyone can be a container gardener. Growing plants in containers brings new colors and design elements into play. Containers are great for areas with poor soil and limited space. They can decorate decks and patios or be placed directly in beds and borders to provide height and other visual effects. Although they need to be watered more frequently than plants grown in the garden, they surely occupy less space, reducing the total amount of water needed to keep them growing. They can be changed out easily for seasonal color and display. And they can be moved about. Herbs are ideally suited to containers, and most garden vegetables thrive in containers.

Container Basics
Container selections have never been bigger or better. The myriad materials include plastic, cement, terra cotta, glazed pottery, stoneware, wood (cedar or redwood are best), and wire.

Adequate drainage is critical for container plantings.

- The hole(s) in the bottom of the pot should be at least ½ inch in diameter.
- Avoid pots that have saucers permanently attached.
- Containers made of more porous materials will lose moisture more rapidly than others.
- Set containers in saucers or on bricks or pot feet, not directly on a surface, to allow for drainage and discourage ants from finding their way into the container.

Consider the **size requirements**.

- Containers should be sufficiently large to allow for root growth.
- Large plants and tall plants

need ample weight for stability.

- Large containers retain moisture longer than small ones, but root rot is a threat if the soil becomes waterlogged.
- Appropriate size is especially important when growing vegetables.

The extra space of oversized decorative containers can be filled with packing material, although static electricity or working with the material on a windy day may be a challenge. Eventually it will break down and need to be replaced. Rocks, in most cases, are just too heavy. Planting in a smaller container and placing it on a perch (an inverted pot works well) inside the large container is a good way to take care of extra space. There are products, for example, Better Than Rocks, made from spongy recycled plastic that can be cut to size. Whatever you use, a layer of landscape fabric between the filler and the soil mix will prevent the soil from filtering down into the filler but still allow for drainage.

Soil mix used for container plantings must be well aerated, be well drained, and retain moisture. Unless very well amended, garden soil loses these essential properties over time and is not recommended for use in containers. Garden soil may also harbor insects, weeds, and diseases. Perlite, vermiculite, peat, and bark are the main components of many so-called soil-less mixes and should always be moistened before using. They may be reused until they no longer drain well or become compacted. Old mix is a great addition to the compost pile.

As in the garden, you need to know your plants' **watering needs** and select and group accordingly. The most fabulous container garden will come only to grief if its components are incompatible.

- Water sufficiently to moisten the entire soil ball, until some runs through the container. Soil mixes with a high peat content are devilishly difficult to rewet once allowed to completely dry out.
- Soil mixes with polymer products (crystals that turn into water-holding gels once moistened) retain water longer and reduce watering frequency.
- Don't water automatically; check with your finger to determine the need for water.

Fertilizing is necessary when you use soil-less mixes, which, unless stated on the package, have no nutrient value. The container gardener is responsible for providing all plant nutrition.

- Liquid and slow-released pelletized fertilizers are preferred for container-grown plants. Granular fertilizer may result in salt accumulation in the soil.
- Use formulations, amounts, and frequencies recommended on the fertilizer labels.

Growing vegetables and herbs in containers saves space and allows you to follow the sun, if necessary. Containers need not be fancy—gallon jugs and old baskets will do nicely. Size is important, though, and 5-gallon plastic plant containers are good for growing most vegetables.

Vegetable Varieties for Container Gardens

Cucumbers: Burpless, Crispy, Early Pik, Liberty, Salty

Eggplant: Black Beauty, Florida Market, Long Tom

Green Beans: Contender, Greencrop, Topcrop; pole: Blue Lake, Kentucky Wonder

Green Onions: Beltsville Bunching, Crystal Wax, Evergreen Bunching

Leaf Lettuce: Bibb, Buttercrunch, Dark Green Boston, Ruby, Romaine, Salad Bowl

Parsley: Evergreen, Moss Curled

Peppers: Canape, Keystone Resistant Giant, Yolo Wonder; hot: Jalapeño, Red Cherry

Radishes: Cherry Belle, Scarlet Globe; white: Icicle

Squash: Dixie, Early Prolific Straightneck, Gold Neck; green: Diplomat, Senator, Zucco

Tomatoes: Patio, Pixie, Saladette, Small Fry, Spring Giant, Tiny Tim, Toy Boy, Tumbling Tom

 **FYI: Container Gardening**

Texas A&M University Floriculture Program (http://aggie -horticulture.tamu.edu/floricul ture/container-garden/index .html). This nice site from A&M is geared to the professional but has lots of great information for anyone interested in growing plants in containers, including hanging baskets. The excellent photo gallery is a wonderful place to see what combinations work well together. Design principles, color theory, and container gardening tips are all here.

University of Illinois Extension Successful Container Gardens (http://urbanext.illinois.edu/ containergardening/default.cfm). A good, comprehensive site with helpful videos.

Vegetable Gardening in Containers (http://aggie-horticulture. tamu.edu/extension/container/ container.html). Here is a simple, no-frills site that has all the basics you need to know.

 **FYI: General Landscape & Garden Design**

Aggie Horticulture Home Landscape Design (http://aggie-horti culture.tamu.edu/lawn_garden/ landscape.html). This site is good on basics and provides links to regional gardening styles, fact sheets, and other publications.

Garden Conservancy Open Days (http://www.gardenconservancy .org/). This is the best show in town for viewing outstanding area gardens. A national organization, the Conservancy is dedicated to preserving exceptional

American gardens. Central Texas gardens are presented every other year, usually in early fall. Check the Web site for the annual schedule and don't miss the tour.

Many local garden organizations also hold open days. Contact the organization directly, or ask your extension agent for information.

The Landscape Design Site (http://www.the-landscape-de sign-site.com/). This commercial megasite offers information on every aspect of landscaping. Its many helpful how-to videos are clear and uncomplicated.

Monrovia (http://www.monro via.com/design/). The giant plant grower's very attractive Web site offers step-by-step instructions for making a landscape plan. The how-to videos and plant catalog with superb photos are very well done. A most helpful feature is the suggested companion plants for each listed plant.

CHAPTER 5

Lawns and Turfgrasses for Central Texas

ONCE THE CENTER of the home owner's pride, the Great American Lawn currently is being reconsidered. It is now seen by many as an insatiable water hog, an evil monoculture, a major polluter from pesticide runoff and gasoline-powered equipment, and finally, a weekend tyrant by those who still mow their own. Wow, a far cry from the lofty ideals that inspired Frederick Law Olmsted, America's revered nineteenth-century landscape architect,

and others to promote the lawn as a means to improve the appearance of a young America's dismal-looking urban and rural landscapes. A vast greensward uniting neighbors and communities was viewed as a reflection of the new country's democratic values of openness and neighborliness. This ideal was refined and advanced throughout the twentieth century.

Today, Texas lawn care is a multibillion-dollar business, with single-family homes accounting for 58 percent of the managed turfgrass. Home owners use many times the amount of pesticides per acre on their lawns as farmers do on their farms. The average single family home requires forty hours of mowing annually—one hour of mowing consumes the amount of gas used to drive twenty miles.

So why are many of us still out there mowing, watering, and fertilizing? What does a lawn do for us? It tolerates foot traffic like no other living plant material. It cools the area physically and psychologically, absorbs noise, stifles weeds, filters water and air pollutants, and contributes oxygen to the atmosphere. Its uniform smooth texture makes an excellent background material for trees, shrubs, and other design elements. Finally, deer don't eat it! All of these reasons make a good case for turfgrass as a valuable feature in our home landscape, but water shortages due to drought and growth demand that we use turfgrass more imaginatively and conservatively than before. No doubt there will be high-performing dwarf grass and better drought-tolerant varieties suitable for turfgrass in our future (Lady Bird Johnson Wildflower Center has a pilot project to develop a multispecies turfgrass with just such attributes), but at this time we should no longer let the Great American Lawn be our default landscape. New focus on rethinking how much lawn we really need and proper lawn care is essential for responsible twenty-first-century Central Texas home landscapes.

Turfgrass Varieties for Central Texas

Our four Central Texas turfgrasses are categorized as warm-season grasses. They begin growing in mid- to late spring and continue through midfall. Ideally, all should be planted early in the fall or late winter to early spring. It is important to avoid midsummer planting, when plant stress and water use are at their highest.

St. Augustine (*Stenotaphrum secundatum* (Walt.) Kuntze) is native to the Atlantic coasts of Africa and Latin America and along the Gulf of Mexico. It is favored for its dense, thick turf, which crowds out weeds and other grasses. The most shade tolerant of our turfgrasses, its broad leaves remain green long into the season, all year if the weather is mild. 'Raleigh,' the most commonly used variety, is cold tolerant and resistant to St. Augustine decline (SAD), a viral disease, but is susceptible to chinch bugs. 'Floratam' (developed by the Texas and Florida agricultural experiment stations) is a fast-growing and vigorous variety. It is resistant to both SAD and chinch bugs but is less cold tolerant than 'Raleigh.' The semi-dwarf 'Seville' is also SAD and chinch bug resistant but lacks cold tolerance.

St. Augustinegrass *(Stenotaphrum secundatum* (Walt.) Kuntze)

Bermudagrass (*Cynodon dactylon*) is known as "the sports turf of the South," and, as you would expect, this vigorous grass holds up extremely well under heavy use. Deep roots help prevent soil erosion and make it drought tolerant. Its toughness makes it an ideal choice for playgrounds, parks, and golf courses as well as home lawns. One might say that bermudagrass knows no bounds. The most common complaint is its invasiveness in vegetable gardens and flower beds. Common bermudagrass can be sown, but all hybrids such as 'Tifway' and 'Tifgreen' must be sodded. It requires full sun to perform at its best.

Bermudagrass *(Cynodon dactylon)*

Zoysiagrass (*Zoysia japonica*) is a native of Asia and is also known as Korean or Japanese lawn grass. With proper care, zoysia makes an attractive turf that resists invasion by weeds and other grasses, as well as damage from insects and disease. Zoysia has a deep root system that allows it to survive droughts. It is very tolerant of foot traffic. Zoysia does not do well in dense shade. Since it spreads slowly, it is not readily a pest in gardens, but if and when it does begin to encroach, constant care is needed to keep it out of beds. It generally turns brown with a frost and stays straw-colored all winter. More expensive than St. Augustinegrass and bermudagrass, it has become more economical as it has gained popularity. The newer varieties of zoysia—'Emerald,' 'El Toro,' and 'Palisades'—require less water than old varieties and are more shade tolerant. While zoysia will do just fine mowed with a rotary mower, perfectionists prefer to use a reel mower for a more polished appearance.

Buffalograss (*Buchloe dactyloides*) is a native grass of the Great Plains. Finely textured and bluish gray, it looks great in meadow plantings interspersed with wildflowers. It needs four to six hours of sun. Initial home owner experience with buffalograss in the 1980s was disappointing. Because it was sold on claims of slow growth, extreme heat and drought tolerance, and disease resistance, home owners believed that a little pampering with supplemental water in the summer would make the grass grow just a little thicker and stay a bit greener. They did not realize that they were setting up perfect conditions for a bermudagrass invasion. Buffalograss thrives on neglect and does not require fertilizer. It can be mowed to 2 to 3 inches or left at its mature height of 4 to 6 inches. A common buffalograss lawn can be started from seed, but sod or plugs are

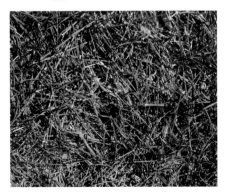

Zoysiagrass *(Zoysia japonica)*

Buffalograss *(Buchloe dactyloides)*

used for the newer varieties: '609' is a rich blue-green of medium density and has a quick rate of growth; 'Prairie' is apple green, is slow growing, and performs well in clay soils; 'Stampede,' a semi-dwarf growing to 4 inches, is the fastest-growing buffalograss variety and has medium density. Buffalograss is best used in lawns with low traffic. It does not tolerate heavy use well, so if you have pets or children who spend time in the yard, another turfgrass would be a better choice. See table below for characteristics of these four turfgrasses.

ESTABLISHING A NEW LAWN

- Clear the area of all debris and existing vegetation. Weeds and other unwanted plants can be removed either mechanically or chemically with a glyphosate, nonselective, broad-spectrum systemic herbicide. Trade names to look for include Finale, Roundup, and Rodeo.
- Level the area to make sure that it doesn't slope toward the house or other buildings on the property. Fill in low spots to ensure good drainage, a must to prevent fungal disease. Leave the

CENTRAL TEXAS TURFGRASS CHARACTERISTICS

Grass Species	Shade Tolerance	Water Requirement	Traffic Tolerance
Bermuda	Very low	Medium to low	High
Buffalo	Medium	Very low	Medium
St. Augustine	High	Medium	Low
Zoysia	Medium to high	Medium	High
Grass Species	Cold Tolerance	Salinity Tolerance	Disease Potential
Bermuda	Medium	Medium to high	Medium to low
Buffalo	High	Low	Low
St. Augustine	Low	Medium	High
Zoysia	High	Medium to high	Medium to low

Source: From http://aggie-turf.tamu.edu/answers4you/selection.htm.

soil level 1 inch below sidewalks and driveways.

- Do a soil test and comply with recommendations.
- Till or loosen the soil and incorporate compost.
- Measure and order the sod. You will want to get the sod on the ground as soon as it arrives, so be sure you and the delivery people are on the same calendar page.
- Start the installation at the drive and walkways because the edges of the sod will be less likely to dry out during the installation. Be sure there is always good contact between soil and sod.
- Water immediately after installation and then once daily for the next two weeks. When the sod seems to be taking hold, begin watering on a less frequent schedule. Soil should be moist but not wet.

Do-It-Right Lawn Maintenance

Maintaining a healthy lawn is not really very hard. When you understand why and how to aerate, fertilize, mow, and irrigate, chores have meaning and pay off with a better-looking and healthier lawn. Proper lawn maintenance means less pollution, less chemical use, and improved water conservation. Maintenance begins in spring, just after the grass has begun to grow.

Aeration loosens compacted soil and improves conditions for soil life. It is done with a lawn aerator, a heavy machine that requires some strength and a good-sized vehicle for transport. It has hollow tines on a heavy roller that pull out 3-inch plugs of sod as the machine passes over the lawn. Aerating can be done at any time, but a good way to start off the spring season is to aerate, fertilize, and water in the fertilizer. For maximum effectiveness the soil should be soft. Water the lawn the night before you aerate so the soil is damp but not soggy. This will permit the aerator's tines to penetrate more easily and deeply. If you have a sprinkler system, flag all the sprinkler heads and station boxes to avoid disastrous contact between them and the aerator. If children or pets use the lawn heavily, aerate annually. If it is lightly used, every other year, even three, will be fine. The difference aeration makes will amaze you. Together, aeration and mulching grass clippings can reduce the amount of fertilizer needed by a third to a half of the recommended rate.

Fertilizing your lawn once or twice a year is adequate (years ago three applications were recommended). The first application should be after the first or second necessary mowing in spring; the second in late September to mid-October. Turfgrass experts recommend a soil test every three years or so, but we all know that most of us skip this step, buy the bag of fertilizer, and just get on with it. One-half pound of nitrogen per 1,000 square feet is recommended for lawns that get light to medium traffic. More heavily used lawns definitely should get a second application in fall. Do not fertilize during drought conditions.

Organic fertilizers are naturally slow-release, which means they are available to the grass over a period of time and are less likely to wash off in a heavy rain. If you use synthetic products, make sure some of the nitrogen is in slow-release form. Because most Central Texas soils are high in phosphorus, make sure your fertilizer has a low "P" number (the middle number in the N-P-K ratio). Water well but not to the point of runoff after applying fertilizer. Avoid weed-and-feed products.

Mowing is not just for appearance. Although few of us are aware that we are doing more than tidying up, proper mowing frequency and height promote grass plant health and can conserve water. The first mowing of the season should be at a low mower setting but *not* the lowest. Years ago we were instructed to "scalp" the lawn, but this practice is now thought to be unnecessary, or even do more harm than good. You want to remove dead grass leaves but not injure the stolons or overexpose the grass or soil.

- Start with a sharp blade and keep it sharp throughout the season. It's important to make a clean, sharp cut, not a ragged tear. Torn edges will yellow, lose more moisture, and become portals for fungus and other diseases. Sharpening is easy to do at home. Blade-sharpening kits are readily available in hardware and home-improvement stores. Be sure the kit includes a balance. An unbalanced blade can do heavy damage to the mower engine.
- Mow at the right height. Different turfgrasses have different optimum mowing heights.

MOWING REQUIREMENTS

Grass Species	Mowing Frequency	Mowing Height (inches)
Bermuda	3–7 days	1.0–1.5
Buffalo	7–14 days	2.5–3.0
St. Augustine	5–7 days	2.5–3.5
Zoysia	7–10 days	1.0–1.5

- Do not remove more than one-third of the length of the grass blade. This is important for two reasons: (1) mowing the grass too low will limit the leaf area necessary for photosynthesis and plant vigor; (2) all grass plants have "growing points" located near ground level from which the leaves emerge. As the grass grows taller, the growing point will rise off the ground. If you remove more than one-third of the blade, you risk taking the growing point, too, resulting in injury or death of the grass plant, so frequent mowings are recommended. In summer when the grass is growing rapidly, you may want to mow more often than once a week. Grass growing in shady areas should be cut at a higher level than grass growing in full sun. The grass needs the full benefit of all the sun it receives.

Efficient watering becomes evermore important as demand for water grows, and extreme heat and mandatory watering schedules have become the rule, not the exception. While automatic sprinkler systems are a great improvement over the seemingly random and uneven applications by hose-end sprinklers, they, too, require regular servicing if they are to be as efficient as possible. Occasional watering may be necessary during winter. Remember that in winter the grass is dormant, not dead.

When should you water? Early morning is the best time to water. If you have an automatic system, set it for 3 AM–4 AM. At this time less water will be lost to evaporation. You can water in the evening throughout summer, but in September, as nighttime temperatures begin to fall, wet grass at night is vulnerable to fungal diseases. Most of all, avoid watering midday.

How much should you water? To maintain healthy grass, you want the soil moist 4 to 6 inches deep. To achieve this, you will need to deliver ½ to 1 inch of water per week. This means, approximately, watering for thirty minutes to one hour, depending on soil type and slope. If there is a slope to your lawn, you will need to check for runoff.

How frequently should you water? Turfgrass experts agree that less frequent, longer waterings promote a deeper root system that will be able to cope better under drought conditions than a lawn that sports a very lush top growth but is supported by shallow roots. To help condition your lawn for drought, you should water only when the first signs of stress occur: bluish bronzy color or footprints that remain in the lawn and leaves that curl.

Turfgrass Troubles

A well-maintained lawn of the correct turfgrass for your site is the best defense against most lawn troubles. Dense turf easily outcompetes most weeds, and proper watering practices can prevent fungal diseases and keep insect populations in check. But occasionally problems do emerge and require attention.

Weeds are best controlled when they are few and before they have gone to seed. Weeds will pull out more easily if the soil is moist. Think Zen when weeding—it is relaxing, it requires no thinking so your mind is free to go where it likes, and it is better for the environment than a chemical solution, which should be your last resort. Pesticides not only pollute waterways from runoff but can damage soil health as well. Avoid using weed-and-feed products that contain both fertilizer and weed killers. They are usually overkill, wasteful, and expensive. Why spread chemicals on every inch of the lawn if you have only a few patches of weeds? The best times to fertilize and kill weeds often do not coincide in Central Texas. Should you decide herbicides are necessary, identify the weeds and then select the appropriate product. There are annual weeds and perennial weeds, cool-season weeds and warm-season weeds, grassy weeds and broad-leaved weeds. Each calls for a different treatment. Ah, the case for prevention is building! Corn gluten is a natural alternative to synthetic herbicides. Classified by the Environmental Protection Agency (EPA) as a "minimum risk pesticide," it works by inhibiting root formation of germinating plants. Corn gluten (9 percent nitrogen by weight) must be applied at the right time and under the right weather conditions to be effective. Two applications, one in spring and another in fall, are recommended. Effectiveness of all weed killers depends on rate of application, timing, soil type, and water. Whatever your choice, read and follow directions carefully.

Insects can also be prevented by good watering and fertilizing practices and good drainage. Chinch bugs, white grubs, and fire ants are familiar insects that cause problems in Central Texas.

Chinch bugs can be found in bermudagrass but are more common in St. Augustine. They are ⅛ to ⅕ inch long, black and white, and likely to appear in dry, sunny areas during the summer. They create uneven patches of dead or yellowing, dying grass. Affected areas are irregularly shaped and can be mistaken for "take-all patch." The test for chinch bugs is to remove both

ends of a metal can, insert one end in the soil, and fill with water. If chinch bugs are in the lawn, they will quickly surface.

White grubs are the larval form of June bugs and are a major treat for armadillos. June bugs eat the grass roots in spring and fall, causing the grass to weaken and die. A variety of synthetic pesticides can be used. Beneficial nematodes are available as a nonchemical treatment.

Fire ants can really prevent you, and especially your children and pets, from enjoying your yard. They are difficult to control because they have the habit of just moving on when disturbed. They can be treated with contact insecticides or broadcast baits (see more on fire ants in chapter 13).

Diseases are most likely to occur in turfgrass during periods of high humidity (this includes overwatering) or where drainage is poor. Maintaining good soil health is the key to prevention. Just as many of our own illnesses start out with identical symptoms such as fever, headache, and chills, a lot of lawn fungal diseases begin with weakening and yellowing leaves that eventually die. If you have difficulty distinguishing the symptoms, your county extension agent can help. Photos and samples will be helpful in making a diagnosis. Brown patch and take-all patch are our most common diseases.

St. Augustine decline, once quite common, has been largely under control since the introduction of SAD-resistant varieties such as 'Raleigh,' the most commonly used variety for Central Texas.

Brown patch starts with small circles of weakened grass that grow ever larger. It usually appears in spring or fall after rain. A key identifying factor is leaves that can be pulled easily from the stolons, the horizontal stems that creep along the surface of the ground or just below.

The first sign of **take-all patch** is yellowing leaves and dark roots. Affected areas may be up to 20 feet in diameter. It is notoriously difficult to control, and although chemical controls exist, their effectiveness is spotty and dependent on application rate, timing, and watering. As with all chemical use, it is vital to follow instructions precisely. Often fungal damage is corrected with a dose of compost to the affected area and a bit of time. The compost acts by bringing soil microbial life into balance as it decomposes. Of course, it is better and easier in the long run to concentrate on prevention.

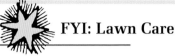 **FYI: Lawn Care**

AggieTurf (http://aggie-turf.tamu.edu/answers4you/) provides complete information about lawn care in Texas. The site's excellent calculators for water and fertilizer applications and sod measurements take the guesswork out of irksome chores. All major Texas lawn topics are treated in depth. The excellent photos are helpful with diseases and insect damage.

Alternatives to Lawns: Ground Covers and Accent Plants

THE GROWING popularity of alternatives to lawn is a welcome and exciting change in landscape design, introducing many new plants and sparking our imaginations. Four reasons driving their success are our increased awareness of the need to conserve water by reducing the area in turfgrass, the trend toward smaller residential lots, the desire for lower-maintenance yards, and interest in more sophisticated design.

Alternatives may be traditional ground covers, such as liriope and Asian jasmine; or nonshrub accent plants such as ferns, ornamental grasses, agaves, and yuccas. Hardscape, or nonliving materials like stone, wood, and decomposed granite, comprise an increasing share of the home landscape. These alternatives with their varied colors, forms, and textures have given a new look to our urban and suburban landscapes. And they have more than aesthetic value—they are effective and efficient problem solvers for many situations.

Traditional Ground Covers

Loosely defined, **traditional ground covers** are nonshrub plants 18 inches or less in height. They are used often where turfgrass is difficult to grow: places that are too shady, steep slopes, and small or irregularly shaped areas where standard lawn maintenance is awkward are ideally suited for ground covers. They are excellent at controlling erosion and retarding weeds. The varied sizes, colors, and textures of ground covers heighten visual interest by defining spaces, softening the appearance of drives and walks, and providing a transition between other landscape elements.

When selecting ground covers, as always, consider soil conditions, exposure, and moisture requirements. Growth rate and whether the plant is evergreen or deciduous are other important details to know. We all want quick coverage, but the line between acceptable growth and outright invasion is very fine. Once charmed by the dappled leaves and perky early blooms of the creeping buttercup (*Ranunculus repens*) and the promise that it would thrive in sun or shade, I bought three 4-inch plants. What a disaster a year or two later. Creeping buttercups were everywhere—in the lawn, the vegetable garden—and no longer so charming. Had I done my homework before buying, I would have discovered that it was high on the invasive weed list and saved myself a lot of work.

Ground covers have two significant limitations: they do not tolerate foot traffic well, and even a fast-growing ground cover requires at least two years of a conscientious fertilizing, watering, and weeding regimen to become well established and provide good coverage.

Preparation, Planting, and Care

Spring and fall are the ideal times for establishing ground covers. After you have defined your area and selected the plant material, it is time to prepare the site.

- Level or grade the area.
- Remove existing vegetation by mechanical means, chemical means, or soil solarization. (See "Weed Management" in chapter 13.)
- Rake the area free of rocks and other debris.
- Fork or till in at least 3 inches of compost.
- On slopes it is best to use erosion-control netting secured with garden staples to minimize erosion until the plants are established.

After bed preparation is a good time to install an edger if you plan to use one. Edgers help keep the bed defined and make maintenance easier. Stone, steel, plastic, and wood are popular edging materials. The edger needs to be

How to calculate the number of plants needed: Multiply the number of square feet by the multiplying factor for the spacing you plan to use. Example: To cover 100 square feet with plants spaced 8 inches apart, you would need 220 plants.

Spacing (inches)	Multiplying factor (inches)
6	4.0
8	2.2
12	1.0
18	.44
24	.25
36	.11

installed thoughtfully and carefully: steel edgers can be mower hazards if installed at the wrong height; plastic tends to pop up over time as the soil shrinks and expands.

Planting
- Dig a hole twice as wide as the soil ball and the same depth.
- Stagger the rows to prevent erosion.
- Add an appropriate amount of controlled-release fertilizer such as Osmocote in each hole.
- Water in well.

Now it's time to mulch. Mulching is especially important for ground covers. Because you want them up and growing quickly, the goal is to prevent sunlight from reaching the soil but to allow for air circulation and water penetration. A 2- to 3-inch layer of organic mulch such as bark, pine straw, and shredded leaves does the job well and over time will enrich the soil. Unsightly and impermeable, black plastic does not allow air and water to enter the soil and makes it difficult for runners to root. Woven polypropylene weed-barrier fabric has its supporters and critics. It, too, slows and reduces air and water penetration and, like black plastic, needs to be installed carefully so that puddles are not created in any depressions that may remain on the surface of the soil. After mulching, it is important to water again.

Care
Once established, ground covers require fertilizing, weeding, watering, and mulching. Really robust growers like Asian jasmine or Katie ruellia might do just fine with a dose of compost once or twice a year; less assertive plants will appreciate an application of a complete fertilizer in autumn and once more in early spring,

similar to the requirement for lawns. Water appropriately in spring, summer, and fall and occasionally in winter if there is little rain. Your main chore will be keeping the area weed-free until the area is fully covered. Weed early, when weeds are easily removed from the soil, and often.

Traditional Ground Covers for Central Texas

Ajuga, Carpet Bugle
(*Ajuga reptans*)
Evergreen
Height: 6–10 inches
Spread: 5–10 inches
Growth Rate: Moderate
Flower: Whorls of blue-violet
  blossoms March to April

Soil: Humusy, well drained,
  moist
Maintenance: Low
Comments: The crinkled leaves
  have a handsome bronze cast.
  Color will vary by variety. Set
  plants 6–8 inches apart for
  good coverage. Avoid planting
  in heavy, wet soils where ajuga
  is prone to crown rot. Excellent ground cover for shady areas. The elegant dwarf variety
  'Chocolate Chip' is an excellent choice for small spaces.

Asian Jasmine
(*Trachelospermum asiaticum*)
Evergreen
Height: 6–12 inches
Spread: 36 inches
Growth Rate: Fast
Flower: Rarely in Central Texas
Soil: Adaptable
Maintenance: A nice trim at the lawn mower's highest setting every other spring.

Comments: Dense, robust, and low growing, this reluctant climber is a superb ground cover. The leaves are glossy with a handsome bronze cast. Smaller-leaved and variegated varieties, which do better in full sun, are available. May suffer cold damage in severe winter; otherwise there are no problems.

Cast Iron Plant
(*Aspidistra elatior*)
Evergreen
Height: 2–3 feet
Spread: 1–2 feet
Growth Rate: Slow
Flower: Rare and inconspicuous
Soil: Very tolerant of poor soils
Maintenance: Low to medium
Comments: Flourishing in the
    most difficult environment—
    dry soil and deep shade—this
    broad-leaved member of the
    lily family is often relegated
    to waste places in the land-
    scape. When used more cre-
atively, such as in drifts in the
understory, it is a strikingly
handsome plant. It does, however, have little tolerance for
sun and will sunburn easily.
For best appearance, plant it
where it will be protected from
the wind. Keep it looking fresh
and new by removing dead
and damaged leaves or, better yet, by cutting back all the
leaves in early spring before
new growth begins. 'Milky
Way' is a delightful smaller,
white-spotted variety.

Coralberry
(*Symphoricarpos orbiculatus*)
Deciduous
Height: 1–4 feet
Spread: 1–2 feet
Growth Rate: Fast
Flower: White inconspicuous flowers in spring followed by attractive coral berries lasting through winter
Soil: Adaptable, well drained
Maintenance: Low to medium

Comments: Readily rooting at ground contact, this native makes a nice airy ground cover under trees. Cut back to encourage bushiness and keep it low growing.

Dwarf Mexican Petunia
(*Ruellia brittoniana*)
Evergreen
Height: 6 inches
Spread: 8–10 inches
Growth Rate: Fast
Flower: Purple-pink
Soil: Very tolerant of poor soils
Maintenance: Low

Comments: Thriving under harsh conditions, this low-growing ground cover spreads nicely and has a long blooming season. A very care-free plant.

English Ivy
(*Hedera helix*)
Evergreen
Height: 20–40 feet
Spread: Boundless if not con-
    trolled
Growth Rate: Moderate
Flower: None
Soil: Adaptable, well drained
Maintenance: Medium to high
Comments: English ivy is the
    overachiever of vines. Once
    widely used as an effective
    and versatile ground cover and
    climber, it is now considered
    invasive and not a water-wise
choice. Given that it has attractive foliage, is cold hardy,
and provides good coverage in
very shady areas, English ivy
may be useful in special or difficult situations. It needs little
encouragement, so ivy maintenance is all about control.
Keep it out of trees and out of
the neighbors' yards. **Algerian
Ivy** (*H. canariensis*) has large
6-inch leaves and is a good
choice for dense coverage of
large spaces. Less cold tolerant
than English ivy, its growing
requirements are similar, and
it will tolerate dry periods.

Eyelash Sage
(*Salvia blepharophylla*)
Evergreen
Height: 12–18 inches
Spread: 18–24 inches
Growth Rate: Moderate to fast
Flower: Deep scarlet in early
  summer to early fall
Soil: Well drained, organically
  enriched
Maintenance: Low. Cut back in late winter. Can be divided in late winter, early spring. An application of fish emulsion/ liquid seaweed or compost in spring is optional.

Comments: Flowers have a magical, shimmering, translucent quality. Foliage is dark green. Moderately drought tolerant once established. Hardy to 20°F.

Leadwort Plumbago
(*Ceratostigma plumbaginoides*)
Evergreen
Height: 6–10 inches
Spread: 10–16 inches
Growth Rate: Moderate
Flower: Deep blue flowers in
    summer and early fall
Soil: Well drained, organically
    enriched

Maintenance: Cut back after
    plant has finished blooming.
    Can be divided in late winter
    or spring. Apply an annual
    dressing of compost.
Comments: Has lovely shiny,
    bronze-red foliage in fall. Will
    freeze to the ground in cold
    winters.

Liriope

(*Liriope muscari*)

Evergreen

Height: 6–12 inches

Spread: 8–10 inches

Growth Rate: Moderate

Flower: Violet, lavender, or white in summer and early fall

Soil: Adaptable, good drainage

Maintenance: Very low

Comments: An evergreen, grass-like perennial that forms a dense covering for the ground, liriope produces small white or purple flowers on spikes in summer or early fall. It makes a fine border plant and ground cover under trees. It tolerates heat and drought once established and thrives in soil improved with compost. Preferring semishade, it can suffer sunburn in long exposure to the bright summer sun. Many attractive cultivars of liriope are available, especially variegated varieties such as 'Silver Dragon' and 'Silvery Sunproof.' Possessing the same characteristics, and growing to 3 inches in height and width, 'Evergreen Giant' is a superb choice for an accent in shady areas of flower beds and borders. It looks good with river fern and gingers.

Monkey Grass, Mondo Grass
(*Ophiopogon japonicus*)
Evergreen
Height: 4–5 inches
Spread: 4–10 inches
Growth Rate: Slow
Flower: Lavender spike, incon-
spicuous
Soil: Well drained, organically
enriched
Maintenance: Low

Comments: Smaller and more
finely textured than liriope.
Plant 6–12 inches apart. Once
established, monkey grass
is drought tolerant. **Dwarf
Monkey Grass** (*O. japonicus*
'Nana') is more compact and,
like all dwarf varieties, grows
more slowly to about 3 inches.

Pigeonberry
(*Rivina humilis*)
Deciduous
Height: 1–2 feet
Spread: 1 foot
Growth Rate: Moderate
Flower: Pale pink spikes May
through October followed by
bright red or orange berries
Soil: Moist, well drained
Maintenance: None

Comments: Water this delightful
native in summer to prevent it
from going dormant. A favorite
food of white-winged doves.
Dies back in winter.

Purple Heart
(*Setcreasea pallida*)
Deciduous
Height: 12 inches
Spread: 16 inches
Growth Rate: Fast
Flower: Purple flowers in spring
and summer
Soil: Adaptable
Maintenance: Trim to keep neat.

Comments: Its purple swordlike leaves bring great color and texture to the scene. Spreads aggressively by fleshy roots. Dies back in winter but will be right back up in spring. This plant is excellent at tolerating extreme heat and sun.

Silver Ponyfoot
(*Dichondra argentea*)
Deciduous
Height: 3 inches
Spread: 36–48 inches
Growth Rate: Fast
Flower: Inconspicuous creamy to white in spring
Soil: Well drained
Maintenance: Trim to keep neat.

Comments: Silver foliage and a creeping, flowing habit make this a dramatic ground cover as well as a popular container garden plant. Looks great trailing over walls and rocks. Loves the Texas sun.

Texas Sedge
(*Carex texensis*)
Evergreen
Height: 4–8 inches
Spread: 12 inches
Growth Rate: Moderate
Flower: Inconspicuous green in
    spring
Soil: Moist, well drained pre-
    ferred but very adaptable
Maintenance: None

Comments: Tolerating sun or
    shade, wet to dry soil, this is
    one of the most useful and
    versatile native ground cov-
    ers available. It will also take
    light foot traffic and mowing at
    a high setting, though admit-
    tedly it looks
    best in natural form. Self-seeds
    readily.

Woolly Stemodia
(*Stemodia tomentosa*)
Semi-evergreen
Height: 3–5 inches
Spread: 12 inches
Growth Rate: Fast
Flower: White or violet
Soil: Tolerates poor soil but must be well drained
Maintenance: Shear back in late winter.

Comments: Native to coastal and South Texas, woolly stemodia forms a dense, low-growing mat. It will take all the sun it can get. Excellent in containers where its flowing habit and silvery color are readily appreciated.

Agaves, Yuccas, Cacti, and Relatives Checklist

Agaves are bold, dramatic, and sculptural. Most are native to dry, rocky, poor soils, but they will tolerate rich soil if it is well drained. They thrive on neglect, rarely need fertilizer, and are pretty much pest-free. Agaves can be blue, gray, green, or variegated. They can be huge or small; some varieties are sun lovers, and others are shade tolerant. When shopping for agaves, be sure to inquire about growth rate, ultimate size, and hardiness zones. Many do well in containers, where they can have a powerful visual effect.

Newly planted agaves should be watered every four or five days for the first month or two until they are established. Agaves die after they bloom, though depending on species, that may be thirty-five years or longer. Agaves propagate by sending out offsets or "pups" from the stem base. Because most have sharp spines and can grow to considerable size, placement is an important consideration. Currently enjoying great popularity, new species are frequently being introduced at nurseries. Following is a partial list of striking, hardy agaves for Central Texas.

Agave Striata
(*Agave striata*)
Evergreen
Height: 3 feet
Spread: 3 feet
Growth Rate: Moderate

Flower: Yellow spike to 8 feet
Soil: Well drained
Maintenance: Low
Comments: Unusual stiff, grass-
    like foliage is a lovely gray-
    green hue. Very cold hardy.

Century Plant
(*Agave americana*)
Evergreen
Height: 4–6 feet
Spread: 6 feet
Growth Rate: Moderate
Flower: Purple spike 15–20 feet
Soil: Well drained

Maintenance: None
Comments: One of the earliest agaves used in Central Texas landscapes. Its flower stalk, resembling a giant asparagus, ascends to a height of 20 feet or more and bursts open to expose its yellow blossoms.

Parry's Agave
(*Agave parryi* var. *tuncata*)
Evergreen
Height: 1–2½ feet
Spread: 2–3 feet
Growth Rate: Slow
Soil: Well drained, adaptable
Maintenance: Low

Comments: Gray or green pointed leaves have toothed margins, and the tips are brown to black on this strikingly handsome agave. Size is well scaled for home landscape. Bright yellow flower blooms on 10–15-foot stalk in late spring or early summer.

Queen Victoria Agave
(*Agave victoriae-reginae*)
Evergreen
Height: 1–2 feet
Spread: 2 feet
Growth Rate: Slow
Flower: Pale green to cream spike
    10–15 feet
Soil: Well drained
Maintenance: Low

Comments: Shape is compact, and leaves are dense and artichoke-like with elegant white margins. Has good cold hardiness.

Squid Agave
(*Agave bracteosa*)
Evergreen
Height: 12–18 inches
Spread: 15–18 inches
Growth Rate: Slow
Flower: Creamy white spike
    12–18 inches
Soil: Well drained
Maintenance: Low

Comments: While its delightful, curving leaves are what first attracts your attention, the squid agave has two other unusual and desirable attributes: its leaf tips are soft, and it is one of the most shade-tolerant members of the agave genus. The squid agave may bloom more than once. Provide protection from the burning afternoon sun.

Yuccas

Four yucca species are suitable
for home landscapes.

Red Hesperaloe, Red Yucca
(*Hesperaloe parviflora*)
Evergreen
Height: 2–3 feet, with bloom
    spike 5 feet
Spread: 5 feet
Growth Rate: Slow

Flower: Red or yellow March
    through July
Soil: Limestone based, caliche,
    adaptable
Maintenance: Remove spent
    flower stalks for appearance.
Comments: Stunning yucca-
    like plant looks great in rock
    gardens. Care-free, reliable
    performer. Deer will eat flower
    stalks but not leaves.

Soft Leaf Yucca
(*Yucca recurvifolia*)
Evergreen
Height: 3–4 feet
Spread: 3 feet
Growth Rate: Moderate
Flower: Spike of extravagant

white bell-shaped flowers in summer
Soil: Well drained, adaptable
Maintenance: Remove old leaves and spent flower stalks for appearance.
Comments: A soft-looking yucca with swordlike leaves that bend downward. Attractive gray or green color. Deer will eat flower stalks but not leaves.

Texas Sotol
(*Dasylirion texanum*)
Evergreen
Height: 3–6 feet
Spread: 4–6 feet
Growth Rate: Moderate
Flower: 2–3-foot yellow spike
   June to July

Soil: Limestone based, tolerates
   caliche, adaptable
Maintenance: None
Comments: This evergreen tufted
   lily has leaves more slender
   than those of true yuccas. Its
   trunk frequently is located
   underground, giving the shrub
   the appearance of a clump of
   long grass. Good in rocky
   areas.

Twist-leaf Yucca
(*Yucca rupicola*)
Evergreen
Height: 1–2 feet
Spread: 1–2 feet
Growth Rate: Moderate
Flower: 2–3-foot white spike in
　spring
Soil: Limestone based, tolerates
　caliche, adaptable
Maintenance: None

Comments: Tall white blooms in
　spring. Although deer do not
　eat the plant, they will eat the
　flower stalks. Excellent Xeri-
　scape plant for shady areas.

Cacti

Two cacti species native to Central Texas are suitable for home landscapes.

Lace Cactus
(*Echinocereus reichenbachii*)
Evergreen
Height: 7–10 inches
Spread: 2–3 inches
Growth Rate: Slow
Flower: 2–5-inch intense rose-
  pink in May

Soil: Limestone based, tolerates
  caliche and sand
Maintenance: None
Comments: Because of its small
  size, the lace cactus presents
  best in a rock garden situation.
  The flowers, lasting only a
  day or two, are knockouts and
  well worth waiting for. Plant a
  grouping of three or more for
  greater visual impact.

Spineless Prickly Pear
(*Opuntia ellisiana*)
Evergreen
Height: 5 feet
Spread: 3–6 feet
Growth Rate: Moderate to fast
Flower: Vivid, waxy yellow flowers in May followed by large red fruit
Soil: Limestone based, tolerates caliche and sand
Maintenance: Remove unwanted pads by snapping off at the joint, or, if too thick, cut off with a sharp knife to contain size.

Comments: Cacti always add drama and interest to a setting, and this is *the* prickly pear cactus you want in your garden—stay away from those with spines. Although the spineless prickly pear does not have spines, it does have tiny, finely barbed hairlike spines around the areoles that you will want to avoid. Always wear gloves when working with this plant.

Ferns Checklist

Ferns are particularly useful in shady situations. Their handsome foliage and small to medium size make them valuable accent plants or ground covers. Some are evergreen; others die back in winter. All appreciate moisture and lots of organic matter. Ferns tend to be sensitive to chemicals, so be extra cautious with fertilizer and pesticides.

Autumn Fern
(*Dryopteris erythrosora*)
Evergreen
Height: 1–2 feet
Spread: 1–2 feet
Growth Rate: Slow
Flower: None
Soil: Organically enriched, well drained
Maintenance: Low. Remove old fronds.
Comments: The fronds of this native of China and Japan emerge a beautiful bronze color that later turns olive green. This is a very handsome fern.

Holly Fern
(*Cyrtomium falcatum*)
Evergreen
Height: 1–3 feet
Spread: 1–3 feet
Growth Rate: Moderate
Flower: None
Soil: Organically enriched, well drained
Maintenance: Low. Remove all old leaves in late winter, just before or when new growth begins to emerge, for a fresh, new plant look.

Comments: With rich green holly-shaped leaves, this fern works well in combination with others in shady borders or stands on its own. Although it prefers moist soil, it can be conditioned to tolerate drier situations.

Japanese Painted Fern
(*Athyrium niponicum* 'Pictum')
Deciduous
Height: 1–2 feet
Spread: 1 foot
Growth Rate: Slow
Flower: None
Soil: Moist, organically enriched
Maintenance: None

Comments: Small and delicate, the Japanese painted fern is prized for its striking silvered, almost filigreed foliage. It will go dormant if exposed to hot, summer sun.

River Fern, Wood Fern
(*Thelypteris kunthii*)
Deciduous
Height: 3 feet
Spread: 1 foot
Growth Rate: Moderate
Flower: None
Soil: Very adaptable
Maintenance: Remove dead leaves before new growth in spring.

Comments: Tolerates drier soil than many other ferns but will spread fairly rapidly if given water. Easily divided from root stock. A good, tough, reliable fern for Central Texas.

Ornamental Grasses Checklist

Home owners prize these drought-tolerant plants that work well in landscape plans for reducing the size of lawns. With graceful, arching leaves, ornamental grasses are particularly effective in softening the hard edges of buildings, walks, and driveways. They look good in masses and serve well as accents in perennial gardens. Most of them love full sun and require little maintenance. Trimming back or raking out ornamental grasses in later winter can spiff up appearances but is not necessary. Some are native; others are introduced. The native grasses tend to have a less formal look than many of the nonnatives. Ornamental grasses introduce subtle color, expand our definition of flowering plants, and extend seasonal interest. All contribute striking texture to whatever their setting, and perhaps most delightful of all, they bring movement to the landscape.

Bamboo Muhly
(*Muhlenbergia dumosa*)
Evergreen
Height: 3–6 feet
Spread: 3–6 feet
Growth Rate: Fast
Flower: Pink blooms late summer
through fall
Soil: Fertile, well drained, and
enriched with organic matter
Maintenance: Cut back in late
winter.

Comments: Has graceful, light
green, wispy bamboolike
leaves. This is a great grass for
a soft-looking screen or hedge.
Also good in large containers
at poolside.

Gulf Muhly
(*Muhlenbergia capillaris*)
Evergreen
Height: 1–3 feet
Spread: 1–3 feet
Growth Rate: Moderate
Flower: Pink blooms late summer through fall

Soil: Sandy
Maintenance: Cut back in late winter, if desired.
Comments: Gulf muhly has slender green leaves. This is a great grass for soft-looking, ethereal pink blooms.

Inland Sea Oats
(*Chasmanthium latifolium*)
Deciduous
Height: 2–4 feet
Spread: 2–4 feet
Growth Rate: Fast
Flower: Tan blooms late summer
through fall
Soil: Adaptable
Maintenance: Cut back in late
winter.

Comments: This native has grace-fully arching seed heads and self-seeds easily. One of the few grasses that prefers shade. A good erosion-control plant.

Japanese Maiden Grass
(*Miscanthus sinensis*)
Loses color in winter
Height: 4–6 feet
Spread: 2–4 feet
Growth Rate: Slow to moderate
Flower: Color varies according to variety. Blooms late summer through fall.
Soil: Well drained
Maintenance: Low

Comments: Leaves, flowers, and seeds provide visual interest throughout the year as the seasons change. The many varieties available, including a dwarf, make this one of the most popular ornamental grasses.

Lindheimer's Muhly
(*Muhlenbergia lindheimeri*)
Semi-evergreen
Height: 2–5 feet
Spread: 2–4 feet
Growth Rate: Moderate
Flower: Silver seed heads in fall
Soil: Moist
Maintenance: Remove spent
flower stalks; spruce up with
a rake.

Comments: Grows in gently arching clumps. Foliage is gray or green and finely textured.

Little Bluestem
(*Schizachyrium scoparium*)
Evergreen
Height: 2–4 feet
Spread: 1½–2 feet
Growth Rate: Moderate
Flower: Green, white, and brown flowers June through December
Soil: Adaptable
Maintenance: Low. Cut to ground in winter.

Comments: A dominant grass of the tallgrass prairie, little bluestem is a great choice for a native plant garden. I have admired this handsome native for years on walks in the Hill Country. Stiffly upright and attractive all year long, it is at its most glorious when the blue or gray foliage turns reddish bronze in the fall.

Mexican Wiregrass
(*Stipa tenuissima*)
Evergreen
Height: 1–3 feet
Spread: 1–2 feet
Growth Rate: Moderate
Flower: Green flowers in summer
Soil: Well drained, tolerates alkaline soils
Maintenance: Low. Cutting back old foliage is optional.

Comments: One of our most finely textured grasses, this graceful plant looks great in masses or in beds and borders with others. No grass looks better in a breeze. Drought and frost tolerant.

Purple Fountain Grass
(*Pennisetum setaceum* 'Rubrum')
Semi-evergreen
Height: 2–4 feet
Spread: 2–4 feet
Growth Rate: Fast
Flower: White pinkish plume in summer through fall
Soil: Very adaptable
Maintenance: Moderate. Remove dead growth.

Comments: This large, showy ornamental grass boasts an elegant, subtle purple hue. Easily divided. May not be hardy when the temperature drops below mid-20°F. **Variegated Fountain Grass** (*P. alopecuroides* 'PennStripe'), with creamy white stripes and some shade tolerance, will brighten its surroundings.

CHAPTER 7

Trees and Shrubs: Selection, Planting, and Care

Trees and shrubs are the dominant plant forms in our home landscapes. They are larger, more permanent, and more expensive than most other plant material. They serve many aesthetic and practical functions: form a framework for the landscape; create spaces; and provide privacy, shade, and seasonal interest. Trees and shrubs may be

evergreen or deciduous, flowering or not, tall or short; they may
have fine or coarse texture. In addition, they provide shelter and
food for wildlife, ease pollution,
and shade our homes. These factors should be considered well
before you make a selection.
Do some research; be sure your
future trees and shrubs not only
are appropriate to your needs
but will thrive in their new
environment.

> Consider purchasing larger
> trees from a nursery that
> has a tree-planting service
> available. Often this is the
> only way you can get a first-
> year-of-life guarantee, which
> tells you something about
> how important it is to get
> off to a good start. Besides,
> the nursery workers have
> all the right equipment and
> presumably young, strong
> backs.

SELECTION

- Be sure you can satisfy the
  plant's sun, water, soil, and
  space requirements.
- Select plants with a strong
  form. Avoid buying lop-
  sided shrubs or spindly,
  sticklike saplings, especially

if you buy at the end of the
season. Such plants may
have spent a long time in
crowded conditions with
uncertain care.

- Check for broken branches
  and nicks in the trunk.
- Unwrap and inspect
  wrapped trees for wounds
  or insect problems.
- Look for circling roots. This
  indicates the plant has been
  in its container too long.
  Even though it is best to buy
  trees and shrubs that have
  no circling roots, in truth it
  is often difficult to avoid the
  situation completely. Do not
  buy if the roots look out of
  control. Any circling roots
  should be pruned before
  planting.
- Check the weight of the container. If the container feels
  light, the tree may have had
  inadequate or irregular watering.
- Know the plant's growth
  rate and ultimate size. Trees
  that grow quickly often turn
  out to be short lived and
  weak limbed.
- Be sure to consider the
  tree's year-round appearance. Spring blossoms are
  enchanting and so very welcome after winter, but they
  last only a short time.

TREE SPACING GUIDE

Tree Height (feet)	Minimum Space from Building (feet)
To 25	10
25–50	15
Over 50	20

The Right Plant for the Right Space

Before you start digging, place the plant at the site. Let it sit in its container in the chosen location for a day or two before planting, and ask yourself if the best side is showing, or if it is too close to the house. Remember that trees and shrubs grow out as well as up. You want to avoid blocked views of driveways and traffic signs and potential problems with utilities and air conditioning air flow. Consider how your plant will affect the light inside the house, other plants in the landscape, and, don't forget, the neighbors. It is well worth taking the time. You really don't want to have to transplant in a year or two. It's a big chore, and some trees and shrubs just do not transplant well. Losing a plant from transplanting is always a risk.

Shrubs that fast outgrow their space often require a lot of trimming and pruning. Dwarf varieties are not only smaller but grow more slowly and require less maintenance.

If you select wisely, plant correctly, and follow through on maintenance, your trees and shrubs should flourish and enhance your home for many years.

Planting Trees and Shrubs

Getting new trees and shrubs firmly rooted and properly established in the landscape means less time and resources spent maintaining struggling plants in the future. Planting at the right time and using the proper method for plant type (bare root, balled and burlapped, or container grown) are essential to a healthy foundation for success.

When to Plant
Today most trees are grown in plastic containers, although occasionally you will find very

large or field-dug trees balled and wrapped in burlap. Dormant fruit trees are commonly sold in bare-root condition. These are available in nurseries in late winter and should be planted before the last frost, while still dormant.

In Central Texas you can plant most container-grown trees and shrubs anytime they are available, although you do not want to plant during the summer months. Planting is stressful to the plants; having to cope with heat and drought makes it that much more difficult for them to take hold. September through December are the best months for planting. Roots get established during the fall, and plants are ready to grow when spring arrives.

How to Plant

The following recommendations for planting trees and shrubs will help the plants become established and thrive.

1. Dig a hole *at least* twice as wide as the root ball. Be sure to roughen the sides of the hole with your shovel or a garden fork. If the plant is in a container and does not want to leave it, first cut from the top to the bottom on two sides of the container (a box cutter is a good tool for this

job) and ease the plant out. If the plant is **balled and burlapped** with natural (brown) burlap, do not disturb the wrappings. If, however, the burlap is made of synthetic material (green), all of it should be removed from the root ball immediately before planting, as the synthetic material will not decompose and will restrict root growth. Carefully cut the material away from the root ball. The root ball should be damp to stay intact during the planting process. Center the plant in the hole, and stand back to make sure it is standing straight. Do not rush. Plant the tree at the level it was growing in the container. A discolored ring near the base of the trunk indicates the original soil line. If the plant has **bare roots**, form a cone of soil in the middle of the hole and place the center of the tree atop the cone. Spread the roots out in a natural manner down and away from the center of the cone.

2. Begin backfilling the hole with the same soil dug from the hole. Do not use special soil mix or amendments. The purpose of the large hole, roughing the sides of the

hole, and using native soil to backfill is to encourage the tree or shrub to put out roots and become part of its new environment. Filling the hole with special soil or amendments allows the plant to be content to remain in the enriched, new soil. The roots will not spread, and you will have essentially traded one container for a larger one. By not spread-ing its roots, the tree fails to become anchored and is vulnerable to being toppled by strong winds.

3. Tamp the soil with your feet to eliminate air pockets as you backfill. When the hole is about two-thirds full, fill it with water. If you are plant-ing a tree that is wrapped in natural burlap, untie the bur-lap and gently pull it away from the top of the soil ball after the water has soaked in.

Guy-wire damage on young oak tree

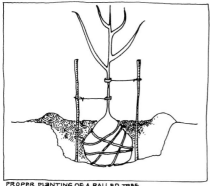

PROPER PLANTING OF A BALLED TREE

Spread it out a bit and leave it to disintegrate in the soil. Finish filling in the hole with soil.

4. Build a ridge or berm of soil 3 to 6 inches high around the perimeter of the hole to form a watering saucer, and fill it with water. No fertilizer is necessary the first year. Remember that if there is no rain, fill the saucer with wa-ter several times a week for the next few weeks. Cover the depression with 3 to 4 inches of organic mulch to preserve moisture and discourage weeds.

5. Some young trees may require support for the first year. Stake the tree to two 6-foot poles with guy wires. Use plastic tubing or garden hose segments on the wire where it touches the trunk of the tree. This protects the tree from the wire rubbing and cutting into the bark. Give the wiring system some slack to allow the tree to sway a bit with the wind. This is how the tree develops its strength and flexibility. The support system should be removed after one year to allow the tree to grow strong to cope with wind on its own.

Special Care Required When Transplanting Trees and Shrubs

Some trees and shrubs transplant more successfully than others. The smaller the plant, the easier it is to remove from its original site without major damage to its root structure. Moving trees with a trunk diameter of 2 inches or more should be left to experts with the skills and equipment to do the job correctly.

Trees with long taproots, such as pecans and oaks, are notoriously touchy and should be moved only if necessary and when the tree is still small. If you must transplant a tree that has a taproot, cut the taproot when the tree is very young and allow the lateral root network to develop and compensate before moving. Transplant in late fall or winter—before the growing season begins. This can be iffy business.

When moving a tree, remember that its root system roughly parallels the spread of its branches and that digging should begin from just outside the drip line. Try to take as much soil with the roots as possible. To achieve this, water several days before you move the plant. The soil should be moist so it holds together well when dug, but not so wet that it will compact when being worked.

Complete transplanting as quickly as possible to prevent roots from drying out. If the tree cannot be replanted immediately, spray the roots with the garden hose regularly and cover to prevent loss of moisture. When transplanting is complete, remove any dead and damaged branches. Do not remove healthy growth. A common misconception is that trees should be pruned to reduce the amount of leaf system the roots support. Pruning healthy limbs removes a valuable source of energy for the tree. Water deeply, mulch, and maintain regular watering for the first year.

Fertilizing Trees

Fertilizing and pruning are the two basic maintenance procedures for trees and shrubs; both are important to young plants. If they are done properly early in the plant's life, the plant will grow healthy and attractive with little need for more than occasional assistance from you.

Some experts recommend delaying fertilizing newly planted trees and shrubs for a year or two. During those early years it is important that the plants get their roots firmly established. Too much nitrogen will promote leaf growth at the expense of the roots. If you feel your soil is depleted, use a light application of a fertilizer low in nitrogen.

Most established shade trees in yards that are fertilized, mowed, watered, and (hopefully) aerated regularly do just fine without additional applications of fertilizer. Lack of terminal growth, many dead branches, and pale or yellowing leaves can be signs of nutrient-deficiency problems. If this occurs, do a soil or foliar analysis or have one done by a professional service. When fertilizing trees, remember to apply under the drip line of the tree, where most root growth occurs. Always water deeply after applying fertilizer. Those who hope for regular harvests from fruit and nut trees need to follow prescribed fertilizing and pruning procedures. Your county extension agent is an outstanding source for that information.

Fertilizing Shrubs

Shrubs require a different approach. Often they are not located in lawns where they would receive regular fertilizer. In sandy and loamy soils the best time to fertilize is in late winter or early spring. In clay soils it is better to fertilize in late fall after the plant is dormant. Because lack of phosphorus or potassium is seldom a problem in Central Texas, a fertilizer with a ratio of 2-1-1 or 3-1-1 is recommended.

Although most evergreen ornamentals require less fertilizer

Do not fertilize trees or shrubs in the heat of summer. The plants are working to survive heat and drought and do not need to be stimulated to put out new growth. Any tender, new green growth put on at this time is vulnerable to freeze damage in winter.

than deciduous plants, maintaining proper soil acidity is a special concern for broad-leaved evergreens such as magnolia and loquat. At the very onset of chlorotic symptoms (yellowing leaves with prominent green veins), these plants should be given applications of iron sulfate or chelated iron. Foliar spraying is the most efficient method of application in this situation.

Pruning Basics

Pruning may be the most misunderstood and mismanaged garden chore. Many of us rarely get beyond a desire to "trim up the yard" before heading out with the pruning shears. Done properly, pruning adds to the health and beauty of our trees and shrubs; however, a poor job can injure, encourage disease, and permanently mar a plant's natural form and beauty.

Heading and Thinning

Two basic training techniques are heading and thinning. **Heading**, or cutting the branches back to just beyond a bud, will encourage new growth at the site of the cut and produce a bushy look, just right for keeping rangy plants in control. It is, however, a method to be used judiciously.

Overuse can alter the shape of a tree or shrub radically.

Thinning is removing an entire branch back to the main stem. This technique opens up growing space and encourages a natural line of growth. Cut close to the outside of the branch collar (the slightly enlarged woody tissue where the trunk and the branch connect). It is important *not* to cut off the collar, for this is where the healing callus will form.

Pruning Trees

Most mature trees need little pruning. There are four reasons for pruning shade and ornamental trees:

- To remove wood that is dead, damaged, or diseased
- To remove undesirable growth that may be interfering with utility lines or other structures
- To improve quality of flowers, fruit, or foliage
- To maintain or reduce plant size

Deciduous trees should be pruned in late winter, when plants are dormant and the framework exposed. However, trees that are inclined to "bleed" heavily when cut should be pruned in summer, not late winter or early spring when the sap begins to flow. **Conifers** should be pruned, if at all, after new growth has been completed but before it has become woody. "Candles," as the new shoots of pines are called, should be cut at about one-half the length of their new growth. The central candle of the top and the branches should be left longer than the side shoots.

PRUNING A LARGE LIMB

Do not top trees unless they are diseased. Topping will destroy the natural growth lines of the trees. Prune suckers at the base and watersprouts on branches. Both forms of growth are easily identified: watersprouts, which are common on fruit trees, shoot straight up off the branches and are different in appearance from other branches. Suckers grow from the roots at the base of the tree or shrub. Both are rapid growers, visually undesirable, and drain energy from the plant that can best be used elsewhere. After pruning diseased wood, wash tools in a 10:1 water-bleach solution before going on to prune healthy branches.

Large limbs should be done in sections; otherwise, prune with the aid of a rope for support. A heavy limb may tear before the cut is completed, stripping the bark and increasing the size of the wound.

Previously, many people believed that wound dressing sealed a cut and prevented damage from pests and disease. This thinking has been discredited by more recent scientific research that has found that wound dressing actually slows the tree's own natural healing process, so it is no longer recommended. **Oaks** are the exception. Blackjack, Shumard, Spanish or Texas red oak, and live oaks are susceptible to oak wilt, a fungal disease spread by nitidulid beetles, and require special pruning care. Prune oaks in the coldest part of winter or the hottest part of summer. Avoid pruning mid-February through June. Paint wounds on oaks with pruning dressing to prevent contagion. Once affected, red oaks can die in a few weeks; live oaks can linger for years.

WHEN TO HIRE A
PROFESSIONAL

Unless you are strong and
agile, have a good deal
of confidence, and have
the proper tools, hire
a professional team to
prune larger trees. Here
the adage "you get what
you pay for" is true. Check
out the credentials and
references of the business.
Get a written estimate, and
ask about insurance and
staff training. Do not pay
before the job is completed,
including cleanup.

Pruning Fruit Trees

When pruning fruit trees, specific knowledge of the tree type
is essential: pruning will affect
the amount and size of fruit produced. Your county extension
agent is the best source of such
information.

Peach. Three scaffold limbs
form a basic network for a producing peach tree. After three
years, remove 40 percent of the
wood annually. Prune the center
most heavily to allow the sun to
penetrate. Unlike many fruits,
the peach does not ripen once it
is picked from the tree, so a California peach in the supermarket
will never compare in flavor to a
Central Texas tree-ripened fruit.

Pear. A pear tree is the easiest
fruit tree to maintain, with the
exception of its susceptibility to
fire blight. It requires no pruning or fertilizing, which would,
in fact, result in excessive, unwanted growth. Light summer
pruning and pinching back of
terminal growth are particularly
recommended for flowering fruit
trees and ornamentals. Done rou-
tinely, these steps can make more
extensive dormant-season pruning unnecessary.

Pecan. Generally, a pecan
tree's central leader is encouraged by pinching off the soft
buds of the side limbs. Branches
growing on the lower third of
the tree should be removed, allowing permanent limbs to grow
at the height of 5 feet. Tip-prune
the limbs by 3 inches in January
through March to encourage new
growth.

Pruning Shrubs

When should you prune? Most
plants can be pruned almost
anytime without having their
survival threatened. However,
there are times that are better for
pruning than others, depending
on species and purpose. **Spring-**

flowering shrubs that form buds during the previous growing season should be pruned right after flowering. Pruning these shrubs later in the year will eliminate next year's blossoms. Shrubs that produce flowers on the current season's growth (mostly **summer bloomers**) can be pruned in late winter. Greater latitude is allowed for **broad-leaved evergreens** (includes all evergreens *except* conifers). These plants can be pruned January through March and again in midsummer, leaving the new growth ample time to harden before the first killing frost. It is best to not to prune in late spring just after

"Crape Murder"

new growth is put on. The plants need this new foliage to restore food reserves.

Frequent, light pruning is better for the health of a plant than long periods of neglect followed by severe cutting back. Many popular ornamentals—crape myrtle, abelia, several hollies, Texas sage, and yaupon, for example—are available in dwarf form. The dense foliage and compact growth habits of these shrubs make them highly desirable in many landscape situations while reducing pruning chores.

Avoid cutting back winter-killed branches prematurely. Gardeners, eager to assess damage and to rid the landscape of unsightly dead branches, often prune plants back to green growth too early after a freeze. The ability of many plants to revive as soon as spring arrives is astonishing and makes such pruning unnecessary. Also, early pruning increases the shrubs' vulnerability to possible late frost damage. Wait until all danger of frost is over or until new growth appears before correcting winter's crimes.

Avoid tapering hedges inward at the base. To maintain fullness at the base of hedges, clip plants at a slight angle tapering *toward* the top of the shrub so that the bottom is a bit wider than the top of the plant. This will allow sunlight necessary for growth to reach the bottom branches.

Geometric shapes, a growing trend in evergreen shrub maintenance, are popping up everywhere. A style that used to be reserved for formal hedges and the occasional specimen shrub is now dotting our landscapes with lollipops, cones, rectangles, and spheres. The species hardly matters; they all look the same. One reason, I suspect, is that it is just much faster and easier for landscape crews wielding power hedge trimmers to zip over the shrubs than it is to work with loppers and pruning shears to encourage and enhance a natural shape. While those perfect shapes do look neat, much richness, variety, and interest are lost when all evergreen shrubs have the same precise and even appearance.

You may have heard of the **Great Crape Myrtle Pruning Debate**. The common practice, particularly noticeable at commercial sites, of severely chopping back the branches of crape myrtles to a few stubs sets some people on edge. "Crape Murder," as the procedure is known to detractors, ruins the natural, graceful appearance of the plant and promotes weak growth. Since crape myrtles are available in sizes ranging from 2 to 30 feet, buying a variety of an appropriate size can reduce unsightly, unnecessary pruning and preserve the plant's natural shape. Crape myrtles should be trimmed back about 20 percent in January to February. Flowers will bloom on the new growth. By removing the seedpods after the first bloom, you can encourage the plant to set out a second round of blooms. This, of course, is much easier to do on the smaller varieties. Keep an eye out for developing suckers, and remove them to maintain the plant's best form.

So let caution be the byword when pruning or even thinking of pruning. Prune only when there is a reason. Some pruning mistakes are terminal. Once a limb is gone, it cannot be glued back. Tempering enthusiasm is difficult on a beautiful day, when it feels so good to be outdoors and working in the garden, but do it. It pays.

 **FYI: Trees**

Arbor Day Foundation (http:// www.arborday.org/trees/index .cfm). An impressive search engine drives a thorough tree guide. Tree basics, including planting and care (videos included), make up just a fraction of this excellent and user-friendly site.

City Arborist Program (http://www.ci.austin.tx.us/trees/default.htm). A treasure of tree information for all Central Texas residents. Contains an "Encyclopedia" link for information on species selection, planting, and maintenance. For Austin residents this site is a source for regulations and legalities (pruning responsibilities, removal, contacts for specific problems) regarding trees within the city.

Cornell Gardening Resources—Trees and Shrubs (http://www.gardening.cornell.edu/woodies/index.html). Available at this Web site are two beautiful PDF publications from Cornell University Cooperative Extension: Information Bulletin 23, *Pruning: An Illustrated Guide to Pruning Ornamental Trees and Shrubs;* and Information Bulletin 24, *The Cornell Guide for Planting and Maintaining Trees and Shrubs.* Both are well organized, lucid, and invaluable. The illustrations are exceptionally handsome and straightforward.

Follow Proper Pruning Techniques, AgriLife Extension (http://aggie-horticulture.tamu.edu/extension/pruning/pruning.html). The how, why, when, and where to prune are all here, including information on specific plants and equipment. Definitely a go-to site.

Trees for Central Texas: A Selection

tilt toward the natives when considering large shade trees. They are adapted to our environment and provide that sense of place. But there are many other handsome trees that also do very well here and enhance urban and suburban landscapes. They may provide an exotic look or dramatic color.

While the distinction between a large shrub and a small tree can be rather fine, trees are usually thought of as plants with single trunks that attain a height of at least 15 feet. However, even with so broad a definition, exceptions do occur. Selected pruning practices can make a difference, too. A listing of small trees and large shrubs follows the shade and ornamental tree checklist.

Arizona Cypress
(*Cupressus arizonica*)
Evergreen
Height: 40–50 feet
Spread: 25–50 feet
Growth Rate: Medium
Soil: Various

Comments: This southwestern native conifer has silver-gray foliage, which is always welcome in the landscape. Its columnar or pyramidal shape makes it an excellent choice for either a screen or specimen tree. This is a very drought-tolerant tree for which good drainage is essential.

Cedar Elm
(*Ulmus crassifolia*)
Deciduous
Height: 80 feet
Spread: 60–80 feet
Growth Rate: Slow
Soil: Adaptable, tolerant of moderately compacted soils

Comments: The small, oval leaves with serrated margins turn a rich gold in autumn.

Honey Mesquite
(*Prosopis glandulosa*)
Deciduous
Height: 30 feet
Spread: 30 feet
Growth Rate: Slow
Soil: Adaptable, well drained

Comments: This handsome accent tree with delicate, fern-like foliage has showy yellow flowers spring through summer. Provides nice contrast to broad-leaved plants.

Pecan
(*Carya illinoinensis*)
Deciduous
Height: Usually 70–100 feet
Spread: 20 feet
Growth Rate: Fast
Soil: Rich, well drained, moist, best in bottomland conditions

Comments: Towering and regal, our Texas state tree is valued for its dignified bearing as well as its nut production. The largest member of the hickory family, this handsome shade tree can grow to 130 feet. It is a fast-growing, deciduous tree with long (9- to 20-inch), dark, compound leaves. The fruit, which ripens in September to October, is smaller and has a harder shell than the familiar papershell commercial varieties (for nut-bearing varieties suitable for our area, see "Fruit Tree Varieties" later in the chapter).

Texas Pistache
(*Pistacia texana*)
Evergreen, semi-evergreen
Height: 20–40 feet
Spread: 25–45 feet
Growth Rate: Fast
Soil: Adaptable

Comments: A hardy native reaching to 20 feet in the dry, limestone-based Hill Country and to 40 feet in deeper, rich, moist soils. The handsome Texas pistache is forgiving of heat, drought, and alkaline soils.

The Oaks

The genus name *Quercus* means "a fine tree." Oaks are a dominant hardwood tree in North America, and Central Texas has its share of strong, handsome candidates for ideal shade trees. Oak tree acorns are a major wildlife food source, but a bountiful acorn crop might happen only every four to ten years. In the following list, Shumard and Texas oaks belong to the red oak group; the others are white oaks.

Bur Oak
(*Quercus macrocarpa*)
Deciduous
Height: 60–70 feet
Spread: 20–35 feet
Growth Rate: Medium
Soil: Adaptable
Comments: Thirty-five years ago a friend at Austin's Natural Science Center gave me one of the large, shaggy-top acorns from which this shade tree gets it species name, *macrocarpa*. Today the tree that grew from it graces the playground of an Austin elementary school with its beauty and shade. A high-branched tree with heavy, spreading limbs, the bur oak has a broad crown and large, deeply lobed leaves.

Chinquapin Oak
(*Quercus muhlenbergii*)
Deciduous
Height: 50 feet
Spread: 20–30 feet
Growth Rate: Fast
Soil: Well drained, tolerates alkaline soils

Comments: This is a good shade tree with few or no pest problems. Its acorns provide food for wildlife.

Lacey Oak
(*Quercus laceyi*)
Deciduous
Height: 25 feet
Spread: 20 feet
Growth Rate: Fast
Soil: Limestone, well drained,
   and rocky

Comments: This smaller oak has
   handsome lobed leaves of a
   gray-green hue and is a good
   choice for difficult sites. It is
   care-free and very drought tolerant, but well-drained soil is
   a must.

Monterrey Oak
(*Quercus polymorpha*)
Semi-evergreen
Height: 70 feet
Spread: 40 feet
Growth Rate: Fast
Soil: Adaptable, moist

Comments: Resistant to oak wilt, this oak is enjoying a surge in popularity as a landscape tree.

Shumard Oak
(*Quercus shumardii*)
Deciduous
Height: 75–100 feet
Spread: 25–50 feet
Growth Rate: Fast
Soil: Adaptable, limestone based

Comments: Closely related to and often confused with the Texas red oak, it grows taller east of the Balcones fault line. A superb shade tree, its leaves turn a lovely red in fall. Subject to oak wilt.

Southern Live Oak, Escarpment Live Oak

(*Quercus virginiani, Q. fusiformis*)
Semi-evergreen
Height: To 50 feet
Spread: 40–70 feet
Growth Rate: Slow
Soil: Prefers poor, well-drained soil, but can survive in clay.
Comments: Live oaks drop their leaves in the spring, usually over a one-month period. Catkins and pollen follow a new flush of leaves, which brings on the caterpillars and grackles. Spring cleanup after the live oaks seems to last forever. But, oh, are they worth it. Nothing says Central Texas quite like the southern live oak.

The smaller escarpment live oak is found in the Hill Country out into West Texas; and the southern live oak, from the Blackland Prairies to the Gulf Coast. Oaks hybridize easily, and often only a botanist can precisely identify the variety. Visit the celebrated Matrimonial Oak in San Saba, Treaty Oak in Austin, and Masonic Oak in Brazoria.

Both oaks are susceptible to oak wilt decline, which occurs in pockets throughout Central Texas. Before selecting the live oak for your landscape, check if oak wilt decline has been a problem in your neighborhood.

Spanish Oak, Texas Oak
(*Quercus rubra* var. *texana,*
Q. buckleyi)
Deciduous
Height: 50 feet
Spread: 15–20 feet
Growth Rate: Fast
Soil: Adaptable, limestone based

Comments: A source of striking red color in fall, this drought-tolerant and generally tough tree is very susceptible to oak wilt.

Small Trees and Large Shrubs

Anacacho Orchid Tree
(*Bauhinia congesta*)
Deciduous
Height: 8–12 feet
Spread: 6–12 feet
Growth Rate: Fast
Soil: Well drained, rocky, lime-
   stone based

Comments: Native to Central
   Texas, this lovely understory
   tree has handsome cleft leaves
   and charming white-pink flowers in spring. If summer rains
   come, it may rebloom.

Crape Myrtle

(*Lagerstroemia indica*)

Deciduous

Height: 25–30 feet

Spread: 25–50 feet

Growth Rate: Moderate to fast

Soil: Well drained

Comments: Who knew! Brought to Europe from the Orient by Marco Polo, the crape myrtle was declared the Texas state shrub in 1997. Apparently unlike the state tree and flower, the state shrub is not required to be a Texas native. Blooming all summer long, the crape myrtle has won the "most popular" title for an ornamental tree. It is available in white, lavender, and almost every shade of pink and red. New cultivars have greatly reduced the problem of powdery mildew so common years ago. The crape myrtle thrives in hot, dry weather. Tolerant of heavy pruning, it has long been the victim of unsightly dehorning, a practice intended to control height and promote a full, bushy top. Left to follow its nature, the crape myrtle will develop into a tall, gracefully elegant tree. With its smooth, pale bark, it can be stunning in the winter landscape. Consult your nursery staff for size, color, and form.

Desert Willow
(*Chilopsis linearis*)
Deciduous
Height: 6–30 feet
Spread: 6–30 feet
Growth Rate: Fast
Soil: Adaptable, well drained

Comments: Another good tree for small spaces, the desert willow needs full sun and good drainage. Its showy pinkish flowers are delightful. Its slightly wild look makes it a good choice for informal, naturalized gardens.

Mexican Plum
(*Prunus mexicana*)
Deciduous
Height: 25 feet
Spread: 10–15 feet
Growth Rate: Moderate to fast
Soil: Adaptable

Comments: A small, deciduous tree, this plum is a southwestern native and has an irregular, open crown. It has fragrant white flowers about an inch in diameter and light green, gently serrated leaves. The dark purplish red fruit varies in quality.

Mock Orange
(*Philadelphus* × *virginalis* 'Natchez')
Deciduous
Height: 10–12 feet
Spread: 6–8 feet
Growth Rate: Fast
Soil: Adaptable

Comments: In Central Texas this loosely formed plant blooms nicely in filtered shade or morning sun. Its white flowers in spring create a romantic mood in evening and when the tree is shaded. It requires annual pruning to retain a nice fountain shape. There are many species and cultivars, including the native **Texas Mock Orange** (*P. texensis*), which grows to 3–6 feet. It has smaller leaves and flowers.

Pomegranate
(*Punica granatum*)
Deciduous
Height: 6–15 feet
Spread: 6–8 feet
Growth Rate: Moderate
Soil: Tolerant of clay and alka-
  line soils, well drained

Comments: Showy orange-scarlet
  flowers in spring are followed
  by heavily seeded fruit, which
  is excellent for fresh eating
  and jelly. Pomegranates prefer
  long hot, dry summers. After
  they have become established,
  they are quite drought tolerant.
  There are several cultivars,
  including dwarf varieties that
  make good container plants.

Rough-leaf Dogwood
(*Cornus drummondii*)
Deciduous
Height: 16 feet
Spread: 16 feet
Growth Rate: Fast
Soil: Alkaline

Comments: Indigenous to Central Texas, this tree has white flowers that are less showy than those of its better-known relative, **Flowering Dogwood** (*C. florida*), which struggles vainly here. In late summer it produces fruit that is relished by at least forty bird species. This fast-growing plant can be shaped nicely with regular pruning.

Rusty Blackhaw Viburnum
(*Viburnum rufidulum*)
Deciduous
Height: 8–20 feet
Spread: 8–10 feet
Growth Rate: Moderate

Soil: Tolerates limestone based, sandy to clay
Comments: This is an extremely handsome shrub with creamy white flowers in spring and waxy green leaves that turn red to orange in fall.

Texas Kidneywood
(*Eysenhardtia texana*)
Deciduous
Height: 16 feet
Spread: 6–8 feet
Growth Rate: Moderate
Soil: Alkaline

Comments: Dogface butterflies, hairstreak butterflies, and bees flock to the citrusy, fragrant flowers. Tolerating the worst of Central Texas' heat and drought, the kidneywood often looks like a lanky, formless shrub in the field, but with a bit of pruning, it can be trained into a handsome small tree.

Texas Mountain Laurel, Mescal Bean
(*Sophora secundiflora*)
Evergreen
Height: 30 feet
Spread: 15–20 feet
Growth Rate: Slow
Soil: Well drained, rocky, sandy to clay

Comments: An extravagant profusion of intoxicating flowers and dark, lustrous green leaves make this informally shaped large shrub or small tree a valuable accent plant. It blooms best in full sun.

Texas Persimmon
(*Diospyros texana*)
Deciduous
Height: 15–30 feet
Spread: 15–20 feet
Growth Rate: Slow
Soil: Well drained, caliche, limestone based
Comments: Slight and delicate with smooth, gray bark and intricate branching patterns, this native has small, leathery leaves and is a desirable accent tree. Its black fruit is appreciated by a variety of birds and mammals. Looks best when not overshadowed by larger shade trees. The messy black fruit can be a nuisance around patios and sidewalks.

Texas Redbud
(*Cercis canadensis* var. *texensis*)
Deciduous
Height: 50 feet
Spread: 25–50 feet
Growth Rate: Moderate to fast
Soil: Well drained, limestone
  based, sand or clay

Comments: Central Texas' favorite spring harbinger displays masses of rose-purple flowers late in winter or early in spring, before it leafs out. Broadly spreading trees with oval leaves, mature redbuds can be good shade providers, although they are planted most often for their early spring blossoms. Several redbud species are available locally. The variety *texensis* does best in our area.

Vitex, Lavender Tree, Lilac Chaste Tree
(*Vitex agnus-castus*)
Deciduous
Height: 10–15 feet
Spread: 8–10 feet
Growth Rate: Fast
Soil: Well drained

Comments: Preferring dry, sunny conditions, this long bloomer produces beautiful spikes of fragrant blue-violet flowers, often used in sachets. Its toothed, lance-shaped leaflets appear in groups of five or more. Multitrunked, it makes a good accent or border plant.

Yaupon Holly
(*Ilex vomitoria*)
Evergreen
Height: 25 feet
Spread: 10–12 feet
Growth Rate: Fast
Soil: Limestone-based sand or
clay; good in drought or poor
drainage

Comments: Slender and usually multitrunked, this native holly is a perfect specimen plant and serves well in many situations. The leaves are small and elliptical; bright red berries are borne on the female in winter. Its curious species name refers to a former medicinal use as a purge.

The **Possumhaw Holly** (*I. decidua*) has a very loose, rangy, almost nondescript appearance during the growing season. In winter, after having shed its leaves, it becomes a glorious standout with a bounty of red berries clinging to it scaffoldlike branches. Possumhaw hollies grow to 20 feet tall.

Hardy Palms for Central Texas

Palms are becoming increasingly conspicuous in the Central Texas landscape, and while they don't exactly shout, "You're in the Hill Country," they can be strikingly effective in the right setting. They look smashing with Mediterranean and modern architecture, and with their large evergreen leaves can be very dramatic with an urban backdrop. Following are some things you should know about palms.

- Spring or summer is the best time to plant palms.
- Palms require good drainage.
- High soil pH can result in nitrogen, potassium, and magnesium deficiencies. Fertilize during the growing season with a slow-release special mix, such as Palm Special.
- Palms should be mulched with a 2- to 3-inch layer, but do not allow the mulch to touch the trunk.
- Some palms, such as *Archonotophoenix* and *Euterpe,* are "self-pruning," meaning they shed their old dead leaves on their own. Others, such as *Washingtonia* and *Syagrus,* require manual pruning. Without pruning, they will develop a "skirt" of old, dead leaves around the trunk, which may become a fire hazard or a haven for rodents. Over-pruning live leaves may cause stress.

Date Palm
(*Phoenix dactylifera*)
Height: 100 feet
Spread: 20 feet
Growth Rate: Moderate
Soil: Adaptable, well drained
Zones: 8–9

Comments: A majestic, stately tree that is hardy to 15°F. Only females produce dates, and only if male trees are in the vicinity to fertilize them. Date production is also limited in cooler climates

Jelly Palm, Pindo Palm
(*Butia capitata*)
Height: 23 feet
Spread: 15–20 feet
Growth Rate: Moderate

Soil: Adaptable, well drained
Zones: 8–9
Comments: Bearing gray-green feather leaves, this palm is very cold hardy.

Mediterranean Fan Palm
(*Chamaerops humilis*)
Height: 5–15 feet
Spread: 5–20 feet
Growth Rate: Very slow
Soil: Adaptable, well drained
Zones: 8–9

Comments: A compact, fan-leaf palm that is hardy to temperatures in the midteens. It is suitable for containers.

Texas Palmetto, Sabal Minor
(*Sabal minor*)
Height: 3–6 feet
Spread: 1–5 feet
Growth Rate: Moderate
Soil: Adaptable
Zones: 7–9

Comments: This is a good understory fan palm. While drought tolerant once established, it thrives in moist forests and bottomlands. This is the palm of Palmetto State Park in Gonzales.

Washington Fan Palm
(*Washingtonia filifera*)
Height: 60 feet
Spread: 15 feet
Growth Rate: Moderate
Soil: Adaptable, well drained
Zones: 8–9

Comments: Dedicated to President George Washington, *W. filifera* is the southwestern native of Palm Springs, California. The fan-shaped leaves are up to 6 feet long and 5 feet across. This palm has small, black, berrylike fruit. It is easy to grow and transplant.

Windmill Palm
(*Trachycarpus fortunei*)
Height: 10–30 feet
Spread: 8–10 feet
Growth Rate: Fast if given regular
   water
Soil: Adaptable, prefers well
   drained
Zones: 7–9

Comments: A fan palm from China, this is one of the most cold-hardy palms. The trunk is covered by a coarse brownish fiber, giving it a distinctive hairy appearance. Good for courtyards or other small or enclosed spaces.

Cycads

Members of this truly ancient group of plants are often mistaken for palms (e.g., sago palm) or ferns, but they are not related. The sago is the most common cycad used as a landscape plant in Central Texas.

Sago Palm
(*Cycas revoluta*)
Evergreen
Height: 10–12 feet
Spread: 4–6 feet
Growth Rate: Very slow
Flower: Male and female plants produce large cones.
Soil: Well drained
Maintenance: Give a balanced tropical fertilizer application in spring. Remove unwanted outer fronds to control size.
Comments: Do not overwater. Sagos produce a new set of leaves in mid- to late spring if grown in sufficient light. Cold hardy to 20°F. Sagos have a strong visual presence. Good in pots.

 **FYI: Palms**

Sun Palm Trees (http://www .sunpalmtrees.com/Cold-Hardy-Palm-Trees.htm) offers an excellent discussion of hardy palms and care instructions.

Fruit and Nut Trees

Full sun, good drainage, and soil high in humus are all crucial to good fruit production, but the single most important condition for fruit bearing is the "chill factor," or the number of hours below 45°F and above 32°F needed to set fruit. Because many fruit trees require seven hundred chill hours, a number much of Central Texas cannot guarantee, selection of varieties proven to produce in our climate is essential.

Most fruit trees in nurseries are "bare root" and should be completely dormant at time of purchase. Buy high-quality fruit trees as soon after they arrive at the garden center as possible. Do not wait for end-of-season bargains—it is crucial that the trees have strong, healthy root systems.

Fruit and Nut Tree Varieties
The following varieties of fruit and nut trees are well adapted to Central Texas.

Apples
Generally apples need more cold weather than the climate in Central Texas provides. However, there are several varieties that grow here, especially in the slightly cooler, elevated or northern parts of our region. You may need two varieties of apples for good pollination.

BRAEBURN
This versatile apple is good for eating, baking, and sauce. It is crisp, sweet-tart with yellow flesh. It keeps for six months or more.

GALA
Fragrant, sweet, and mildly tart, this is an excellent eating apple.

GRANNY SMITH
Juicy, crisp, and tart, the Granny Smith is a favorite baking apple.

RED DELICIOUS
This good eating apple is juicy, mildly tart, and crisp.

Figs
To get a good fig crop, you need to pay attention to soil moisture. The fig tree is shallow rooted and prone to water stress during dry spells, which can result in fruit drop. It is best to mulch and irrigate consistently.

CELESTE

Thriving in all areas of Texas, the Celeste fig is a high-quality fruit for fresh eating or preserving. It ripens in late June.

TEXAS EVERBEARING

The most common fig in Texas, this medium-large fig of good quality ripens in late June. It does best in Central and East Texas.

Peaches

No peach tastes as sweet as a "local" peach, and what is more "local" than your garden? Peach production begins seriously in the third year after planting. Plant the tree in well-drained soil, and keep the soil beneath it weed-free with mulch.

DIXIELAND

A large freestone of excellent quality, this moderately bacterial spot-resistant variety ripens in mid-July.

FRANK

Excellent for canning and freezing, the Frank has been producing consistent crops in Texas since the turn of the twentieth century. The fruit, a nicely textured clingstone, ripens in August.

REDSKIN

Producing in mid-July, the redskin yields a large freestone peach.

SENTINEL

This variety produces a large, semi-cling fruit in early June.

SPRINGOLD

A good early variety, the Springold produces a small clingstone with yellow flesh. It ripens at the end of May.

Pears

With their upright shape and handsome foliage, pear trees are among the most attractive fruit-bearing trees in the home garden. They also are easier to maintain than other fruit varieties. The trees listed here are oriental hybrids that are more successful in Texas than the European hybrids of supermarket familiarity, such as Bartlett and Bosc.

Fire blight is a problem for many pear varieties and can seriously damage or kill trees. Branches and twigs get a blackened, scorched appearance. Affected parts can be cut out (at least 6 inches below the diseased area). Pruning tools should then be cleaned in a chlorine bleach solution. Planting resistant varieties is the best line of defense.

AYRES

This variety is highly resistant to fire blight and produces a medium-sized russet-brown fruit of excellent quality in August.

KIEFFER

A popular variety for canning and cooking, the Kieffer is a great-tasting fresh pear if picked when hard but mature and then allowed to ripen. A hardy species *not* susceptible to fire blight.

WARREN

Highly resistant to fire blight, the Warren produces an excellent dessert-quality fruit in August.

Plums

Small and attractively shaped, the plum tree is a welcome addition to the home landscape. For fruit production it is best to grow two different varieties of plums to ensure pollination.

ALLRED

This small plum has red skin and flesh. Its fruit ripens in early June.

BRUCE

This common commercial variety produces a large, juicy plum excellent for preserves. A pollinator is necessary for crop production.

METHLEY

Self-pollinating and a moderately vigorous grower, the Methley is a good garden variety. This tree produces a medium-sized fruit that ripens in early June.

Pecans

As prized for its stately beauty as for its sweet nuts, the pecan makes an excellent landscape tree if its preferred conditions for deep fertile soil, good drainage, and space can be met.

CADDO

The Caddo has very handsome foliage and produces a small nut of high quality. It begins to produce in five to seven years.

DESIRABLE

A leading commercial (improved papershell) producer of desirable yields of quality nuts. This variety is relatively disease resistant. The tree will bear in eight years.

SIOUX

This yields a small papershell nut of excellent quality. Problems with fungus during periods of high humidity are a possibility.

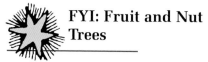 **FYI: Fruit and Nut Trees**

Aggie Horticulture's Home Vegetable, Fruit and Nut Production (http://aggie-horticulture.tamu.edu/lawn_garden/veg_fruit_nut.html) site is invaluable for successful fruit and nut production in Texas. Proper pruning, training, fertilizing, spraying, and weeding practices are necessary for high-quality and consistent fruit, and all the information is here.

Shrubs for Central Texas: A Selection

Central Texans are blessed with a large selection of colorful and interesting shrubs that do well in our soil and climate. There are evergreen and deciduous shrubs, spring- and summer-blooming shrubs, elegant natives and exotic hardy tropicals. Shrubs serve many functions in the landscape. They can define a border or stand alone or in an ensemble to contribute color, form, and texture to a scene. Like everything else, they have their fashion. They may come in or go out of favor for a number of reasons. Some become so familiar that we no longer see them and replace them with newer, less familiar, and therefore more interesting varieties. Others may have been declared invasive, escaping our gardens and competing with native vegetation in our parks and open spaces. Some require too much water for today's emphasis on low maintenance and water-wise planting. Native plants, once the hard-to-find quest of a few devotees, have been hybridized and mainstreamed and are now retailed at big-box garden centers. The following list includes old reliables and newer varieties, natives and adapted shrubs that work well in the Central Texas home landscape without extraordinary care. Many large shrubs are equally attractive and well suited as small trees. These plants are listed in chapter 8.

Agarita, Laredo Mahonia
(*Mahonia trifoliolata*)
Evergreen
Height: 3–6 feet
Spread: 3–7 feet
Bloom Time: Spring
Bloom Color: Yellow
Growth Rate: Moderate
Soil: Alkaline, rocky
Maintenance: Can be cut back to
    maintain size

Comments: This is a terrific plant for those who like the informal look of a naturalistic landscape and are interested in supporting wildlife. Its flowers and currantlike berries provide food for a number of species; the handsome, holly-shaped, stiff, pointed leaves give ideal protection for nesting birds. For the same reason, you will want to plant it away from paths or other areas that get foot traffic.

American Beautyberry
(*Callicarpa americana*)
Deciduous
Height: 3–5 feet
Spread: 3–5 feet
Bloom Time: Spring
Bloom Color: White
Growth Rate: Moderate to fast
Soil: Organically rich
Maintenance: None

Comments: This care-free native owes its popularity to the extravagant profusion of purple clusters of berries from August through November. Birds and animals are known to appreciate their taste as much as we do their beauty. A good understory plant, it prefers filtered light. Flowers and berries grow on the new wood of its elegant arching branches. Nice loose, open shape.

Aucuba, Gold Dust Plant
(*Aucuba japonica* 'Variegata')
Evergreen
Height: 6–10 feet
Spread: 4–6 feet
Bloom Time: NA
Bloom Color: NA
Growth Rate: Fast
Maintenance: Low
Soil: Organically rich, well
  drained
Comments: An easy-to-grow
  plant prized for good perfor-
  mance in shady areas and the
boldly gold-speckled leaves
that give it a tropical look.
The large, tender leaves are
easily burned by the sun; although cold tolerant, it has a
disconcerting habit of turning
black in a heavy freeze. Don't
despair; it will snap back to
life as soon as the temperature rises. Prefers moist soil
but is drought tolerant once
established. Less common but
equally handsome is the solid
green variety 'Serratifolia.'
It produces red berries in
autumn.

Bird of Paradise
(*Caesalpinia pulcherrima*)
Deciduous
Height: 3–10 feet
Spread: 3–12 feet
Bloom Time: Late spring to fall
Bloom Color: Orange to scarlet
    with yellow
Growth rate: Fast
Maintenance: Pod cleanup. Re-
    move frost damage or prune to
    ground in late winter.
Soil: Well drained, adaptable

Comments: Just when the heat of
summer has everything looking dull and droopy, the bird
of paradise bursts into glorious
bloom with airy foliage and
a multitude of large, exotic
flowers. It has finely textured
leaves and a moderately dense
rounded crown. It is reportedly root hardy to 18°F. Other
varieties include the evergreen
Mexican Bird of Paradise
(*C. mexicana*), which has solid
yellow flowers and rounded
leaflets, and the **Yellow Bird of
Paradise** (*C. gilliesii*), whose
yellow flowers have striking
red stamens. The yellow bird
of paradise is the cold hardiest
of the varieties.

Black Dalea
(*Dalea frutescens*)
Deciduous
Height: 1–3 feet
Spread: 2–3 feet
Bloom Time: Summer
Bloom Color: Purple
Growth Rate: Slow
Soil: Well drained, adaptable to clay or sandy, limestone based
Maintenance: Trim to keep dense.

Comments: Charming small shrub with ferny foliage and pealike flowers that attract the smaller butterflies and bees. Looks great in a naturalistic setting. This plant is easy to kill with kindness, that is, overwatering and fertilizer. Cold and heat tolerant.

Boxwood
(*Buxus* spp.)
Evergreen
Height: 4–6 feet
Spread: 4–5 feet
Bloom Time: Spring
Bloom Color: Creamy white, but
inconspicuous
Growth Rate: Slow
Soil: Well drained, adaptable
Maintenance: Shear to shape and
control growth. Apply a gen-
eral fertilizer in late winter.

Comments: Boxwood has been
a popular landscape staple
since colonial times. Its dense,
compact growth and small,
rounded, shiny leaves make it
a desirable choice for hedges,
topiary, and formal landscape
styles. Its shallow roots appreciate good drainage and a light
mulch for protection from the
heat. In a dry winter, water before a predicted freeze. Many
cultivars are available. 'Morris
Midget' is a dwarf variety.

Cape Plumbago
(*Plumbago auricu*)
Evergreen in mild winters
Height: 3–5 feet
Spread: 2–3 feet
Bloom Color: Sky blue
Bloom Time: Spring to fall
Growth Rate: Fast
Soil: Well drained and fertile
Maintenance: Cut back if shrub
   becomes leggy.

Comments: Blooms best in full
   sun. Moderately drought tolerant once established. Has clusters of light blue (a cherished
   color for many gardeners),
   cheerful flowers. Frost tender but returns the following
   spring.

Cenizo, Texas Purple Sage
(*Leucophyllum frutescens*)
Semi-evergreen
Height: 4–6 feet
Spread: 4–5 feet
Bloom Time: Summer to fall
Bloom Color: Pink-purple
Growth Rate: Slow
Soil: Well drained is essential, alkaline
Maintenance: Low. Trim to maintain size.

Comments: The soft appearance of silver-gray evergreen foliage and bell-shaped violet flowers that bloom in high humidity (hence the name "barometer plant") make our state native shrub easy to identify. Shady conditions will result in leggy growth and few blooms. It is often seen as a hedge, but it looks best as a specimen plant. 'Thundercloud' and the green leaf variety 'Green Cloud' are popular cultivars. 'Compacta' is an excellent choice if you desire a smaller, denser plant. Excellent Xeriscape choice.

Chinese Fringe Flower
(*Loropetalum chinense*)
Evergreen
Height: 4–6 feet
Spread: 4–5 feet
Bloom Time: Early spring
Bloom Color: Pink
Growth Rate: Moderate
Soil: Well drained
Maintenance: Feed with acid fertilizer after flowering.

Comments: This member of the witch hazel family produces clusters of radiant, raspberry-colored, frilly flowers in March. The deep reddish leaves are brightest when planted in a sunny location. Mulch to keep roots cool, and prune to maintain shape. Provides year-round interest.

Crimson Pygmy Barberry, Dwarf Japanese Barberry

(*Berberis thunbergii* var. *atropurpurea* 'Nana')
Deciduous
Height: 4 feet
Spread: 2–3 feet
Bloom Time: Early spring
Bloom Color: Yellow, insignificant
Growth Rate: Slow
Soil: Adaptable, well drained

Maintenance: Trim to shape.
Comments: The red-purple to bronze foliage of this attractive, compact shrub looks great when placed close to gray plants and brings a bit of color variety to a green landscape. Has few pest or disease problems but can be susceptible to bacterial leaf spot if not given good air circulation. Has thorns.

Double Bridal Wreath Spirea
   (*Spirea cantoniensis*)
Semi-evergreen
Height: 4–6 feet
Spread: 4–6 feet
Bloom Time: Early spring
Bloom Color: White
Growth Rate: Moderate
Soil: Adaptable, well drained
Maintenance: Thin out old canes
   as needed.

Comments: A lovely old-fashioned shrub, it is recommended for its graceful arching habit and profusion of blossoms.
   It is equally useful as a specimen or an informal, flowering
   hedge. Its small white flowers
   are borne in flat clusters in
   early spring.

Dwarf Nandina
(*Nandina domestica* 'Gulf
   Stream')
Evergreen
Height: 3 feet
Spread: 3 feet
Bloom Time: Spring to summer
Bloom Color: White
Growth Rate: Moderate to fast
Soil: Adaptable
Maintenance: Trim if desired.
Comments: The ubiquitous common nandina has become a
   victim of its own success. With
   colorful foliage and interesting
   texture, and virtually pest-free
and unbelievably easy to grow
under almost any conditions,
it has landed itself on the invasive nonnative plants list. Fortunately, plant breeders seem
to introduce new dwarf varieties with many of the same
positive attributes minus the
negatives at great speed and
regularity. These newer varieties are dense and compact.
They work well as specimens,
in borders, or in mass plantings. 'Harbour' and 'Firepow-
er' are two other attractive and
popular varieties.

Dwarf Yaupon Holly
(*Ilex vomitoria* 'Nana')
Evergreen
Height: 3–5 feet
Spread: 3–6 feet
Bloom Time: Spring
Bloom Color: White
Growth Rate: Moderate to fast
Soil: Adaptable
Maintenance: Trim if desired.

Comments: Thriving in sun or shade, and tolerating many kinds of soil conditions, the trouble-free dwarf yaupon holly is a difficult plant to beat. Excellent candidate for specimen, hedge, or topiary. Try the very slow-growing, compact 'Stokes' variety for small spaces or where finer foliage is desired.

Eleagnus
(*Eleagnus pungens*)
Evergreen
Height: 6–10 feet
Spread: 6–10 feet
Bloom Time: Spring
Bloom Color: White
Growth Rate: Fast
Soil: Adaptable
Maintenance: Trim to shape.

Comments: This large, sprawling shrub has dappled, gray-green leaves with rusty spots on the underside to add color interest to the landscape. It sends out tender, fast-growing canes that will bend to form a spherical shape if left untrimmed. A good, tough specimen or hedge shrub.

Esperanza, Yellow Bells
(*Tecoma stans*)
Evergreen, semi-evergreen, deciduous
Height: 5–10 feet
Spread: 4–6 feet
Bloom Time: Spring to fall
Bloom Color: Yellow-orange
Growth Rate: Fast
Maintenance: Low
Soil: Rocky, limestone based
Comments: Covered with masses of large, yellow, trumpet-shaped flowers late in the season, yellow bells shouts out, "Take me home." Pest-free and extremely heat tolerant, the cultivar 'Gold Star,' developed by Greg Grant, is a Texas Superstar. Other varieties are 'Orange Jubilee' and 'Sunrise.' Esperanza dies back to the ground in a freeze but will return from the roots. Cut back and mulch after the first freeze. Good container plant.

Firebush

(*Hamelia patens*)

Deciduous (evergreen in a mild winter)

Height: 3–5 feet

Spread: 3–6 feet

Bloom Time: Summer to fall

Bloom Color: Orange

Growth Rate: Fast

Soil: Adaptable, well drained

Maintenance: Low

Comments: Sun and heat loving. The late summer vivid orange blossoms are refreshing at a very hot time of the year. Prune to 6 inches above the ground after the first freeze, and mulch.

Flame Acanthus
(*Anisacanthus quadrifidus* var.
   wrightii)
Deciduous
Height: 3–5 feet
Spread: 3–5 feet
Bloom Time: Summer to fall
Bloom Color: Red-orange
Growth Rate: Fast
Soil: Adaptable, well drained
Maintenance: Low

Comments: Flame acanthus has
   an open, rangy habit and can
   get quite large very quickly.
   In full sun the honeysuckle-
   like flowers are profuse and
   very attractive. It may die
   back to the ground in a freeze
   but will return in the spring.
   Low branches resting on the
   ground may root. Very heat
   and drought tolerant.

Glossy Abelia
(*Abelia grandiflora*)
Deciduous to semi-evergreen
Height: 3–5 feet
Spread: 3–6 feet
Bloom Time: Spring to fall
Bloom Color: Whitish pink
Soil: Organically rich, well
  drained
Maintenance: Trim to shape.

Comments: With graceful, arching branches, glossy bronze-cast leaves, and a long blooming season, the abelia is an attractive specimen plant. Responding well to shaping, it blooms on new growth and serves well as a flowering hedge. It responds well to shaping and blooming on new growth and serves equally well as a flowering hedge. Bees love the fragrant flowers. 'Sherwoodii,' a dwarf variety, grows to 3 feet.

Golden Thryallis
(*Galphimia glauca*)
Evergreen
Height: 3–6 feet
Spread: 3–4 feet
Bloom Time: Almost year-round
  if kept warm
Bloom Color: Yellow
Growth Rate: Fast
Soil: Organically rich, well
  drained
Maintenance: Trim to shape.

Comments: Produces very cheerful and profuse yellow flowers on densely leaved branches. Drought tolerant after it has been established. Root hardy in zone 8. Will get leggy if grown in too much shade.

Indian Hawthorn
(*Raphiolepis indica*)
Evergreen
Height: 4–6 feet
Spread: 4–6 feet
Bloom Time: Spring
Bloom Color: Pink-white
Growth Rate: Moderate
Maintenance: Avoid overhead
   sprinkling.
Soil: Humus rich, well drained,
   wide range of soils

Comments: Dark, evergreen, leathery leaves and charming pink-white flowers followed by clusters of blue-black berries. It serves well as a border, in a cluster, or as a specimen and is most attractive when planted in full sun. Good choices for Central Texas include 'Majestic Beauty' and 'Pink Lady.' For smaller areas, try the compacts 'Ballerina' and 'Enchantress.' When grown under less than ideal conditions, it is subject to black spot.

Japanese Yew
(*Podocarpus macrophyllus*)
Evergreen
Height: 10–20 feet
Spread: 5–8 feet
Bloom Time: NA
Bloom Color: NA
Growth Rate: Moderate
Maintenance: Trim as needed
   and fertilize in late winter.
Soil: Well drained, slightly acidic

but adaptable, organically
enriched
Comments: Tall and narrow with
   long, needlelike leaves, this
   bright evergreen adds variety
   of texture and form to many
   landscape plans. Prized for
   its columnar shape, it is commonly used in narrow spaces
   and to soften the corners of
   buildings; however, creative
   pruning and training widen
   the possibilities of this excellent shrub.

Mexican Honeysuckle

(*Justicia spicigera*)
Evergreen (may freeze back to the ground in a hard freeze)
Height: 3–4 feet
Spread: 4–6 feet
Bloom Time: 1½-inch tubular flowers from late winter throughout most of the year

Bloom Color: Orange
Maintenance: Prune back and divide to keep a neat appearance.
Soil: Adaptable
Comments: Hardy to 24°F, the Mexican honeysuckle is a good garden and container plant. It is tough and has good drought resistance.

Oleander
(*Nerium oleander*)
Evergreen
Height: 5–15 feet
Spread: 5–15 feet
Bloom Time: Summer
Bloom Color: Red, pink, white
Growth Rate: Moderate to fast
Maintenance: Prune out unwant-
   ed growth.
Soil: Tolerates poor soil

Comments: Thriving with little attention in hot, dry situations, the oleander boasts flowers of pink, red, or white blooms throughout the summer. Its evergreen foliage is similar to that of the bamboo plant, and it works well as a screen. This plant is poisonous to people and pets and is not appropriate in all situations. It may die in a severe freeze. Dwarf varieties grow to 5 feet and are appropriate for container planting. They are less cold hardy than the standard varieties.

Pittosporum
(*Pittosporum tobira* 'Variegatum')
Evergreen
Height: 10–12 feet
Spread: 8–10 feet
Bloom Time: Spring
Bloom Color: Creamy white
Growth Rate: Moderate
Maintenance: Trim to shape.
Soil: Well drained, adaptable

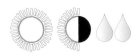

Comments: It's back! Pittosporum suffered great losses in the severe winter of 1989–90, but as our winters seem to have grown milder, it is back again in area nurseries. Dense light gray-green rimmed by white foliage makes it an attractive addition in any landscape. It tolerates pruning well and works in a variety of landscape plans. Left on its own, it will grow to a large size (6–8 feet high by 4 feet wide); 'Wheelers Dwarf' (2–3 feet) is excellent for more confined areas.

Primrose Jasmine
(*Jasminum mesnyi*)
Evergreen
Height: 6–10 feet
Spread: 6–8 feet
Bloom Time: Late winter to
   spring
Bloom Color: Yellow
Growth Rate: Fast
Maintenance: Prune, if needed,
   after flowering. Remove old
shoots to preserve arching
habit.
Soil: Adaptable
Comments: Makes a wonderful
   dense hedge or erosion control
   on a slope. Similar in habit,
   though slightly more delicate
   looking, is the **Italian Jasmine**
   (*Jasminum humile*). Its sweetly
   scented flowers bloom later in
   the season.

Skeleton-leaf Goldeneye, Golden Bush Daisy

(*Viguiera stenoloba*)
Evergreen, mostly
Height: 2–4 feet
Spread: 2–4 feet
Bloom Time: June through October
Bloom Color: Yellow
Growth Rate: Fast

Maintenance: Prune, if needed, after flowering.
Soil: Good drainage is a must. Prefers limestone-based soils, even caliche.
Comments: A pleasant, rounded shape and delicate, wispy foliage to set off the profuse yellow daisylike flowers make this highly deer-resistant small shrub desirable.

Wax Myrtle
(*Morella cerifera, Myrica cerifera*)
Evergreen
Height: 6–15 feet
Spread: 10–12 feet
Bloom Time: NA
Bloom Color: NA
Growth Rate: Moderate to fast
Soil: Sandy
Maintenance: Trim to shape. Apply a general-purpose fertilizer in late winter.

Comments: Graceful arching branches and handsome glossy leaves. Useful as a hedge or small tree. Very tolerant of heat, drought, and poor drainage. Bluish white berries are produced if both male and female plants are present.

Hollies (Ilex *spp.)*

Attractive and serviceable, hollies are available for every landscape. Favorites include 'Burford,' 'Nellie Stevens,' and dwarf Chinese holly.

Burford Holly

(*Ilex cornuta* 'Burfordii')
Evergreen
Height: 10–15 feet
Spread: 5–6 feet
Bloom Time: Spring
Bloom Color: Creamy white
Growth Rate: Moderate

Soil: Adaptable, well drained
Maintenance: Trim to shape.
Comments: There are reasons the Burford holly is one of the country's most popular shrubs: it is good looking, versatile, relatively care-free, and drought tolerant. Its red berries attract birds in winter. A dwarf variety, 'Nana,' is also available. It grows more slowly and is more compact, yet reaches a height of 4–6 feet. It tolerates frequent trimming well. Watch for scale on the underside of leaves and treat with a dormant oil if necessary.

Dwarf Chinese Holly
(*Ilex cornuta* 'Rotunda nana')
Evergreen
Height: 3–5 feet
Spread: 3–4 feet
Bloom Time: NA
Bloom Color: NA
Growth Rate: Slow
Soil: Organically rich, well drained
Maintenance: Trim as needed.

Comments: A rounded form and dense, glossy kelly green foliage make this one of the best-looking hollies. A slow grower, it requires little attention, though it withstands trimming and shaping well. It can be used for a hedge, for a foundation planting, or in mass plantings. Its leaves are spiny.

'Nellie R. Stevens'
(*Ilex* × 'Nellie R. Stevens')
Evergreen
Height: 15–20 feet
Spread: 10 feet
Bloom Time: Spring
Bloom Color: White
Growth Rate: Moderate to fast
Soil: Well drained, adaptable,
    prefers organically rich soil

Maintenance: Trim to shape and
    control growth.
Comments: The small flowers
    are followed by a multitude
    of bright red berries if fertil-
    ized by a male Chinese holly,
    or better yet, by Nellie's male
    counterpart, 'Edward J. Ste-
    vens.' Has better heat tolerance
    than other hollies. Good as a
    hedge, screen, or specimen
    plant.

Sumac *(Rhus spp.)*

Three native sumacs add color and texture to our landscape. They all like sun but will tolerate partial shade.

Evergreen Sumac (*Rhus virens*)
Semi-evergreen (Like the southern live oak, it carries its leaves through winter and then drops them all at once.)
Height: 8–10 feet

Spread: 6–8 feet
Bloom Time: Summer to fall
Bloom Color: White
Growth Rate: Slow to moderate
Maintenance: Low
Soil: Adaptable
Comments: Excellent for all kinds of wildlife, this native can serve as a good hedge if grown in full sun. It makes a nice specimen plant in a naturalistic setting.

Flameleaf Sumac
(*Rhus copallina*)
Deciduous
Height: 8–20 feet
Spread: 10–15 feet
Bloom Time: Summer
Bloom Color: Yellow, green
Growth Rate: Fast
Soil: Thrives in poor soils
Maintenance: None

Comments: This native gives us some of our best fall color and provides food for many birds and mammals. Excellent for large native landscapes.

Fragrant Sumac
(*Rhus aromatica*)
Deciduous
Height: 8 feet
Spread: 4–5 feet
Bloom Time: Spring
Bloom Color: Yellow
Growth Rate: Moderate
Soil: Tolerates limestone based,
     sandy to clay
Maintenance: None

Comments: Three-lobed green
     leaves turn orange to red in
     fall. Leaves produce distinc-
     tive fragrance when crushed.
     Looks best when grown in full
     sun. Produces fuzzy little red
     berries much enjoyed by wild-
     life.

*Viburnum (*Viburnum *spp.)*

Three attractive members of the very large viburnum family do well here, and each makes a distinctive addition to the landscape.

Sandankwa Viburnum

(*Viburnum suspensum*)
Evergreen
Height: 5–10 feet
Spread: 5–10 feet

Bloom Time: Early spring
Bloom Color: Creamy white
Growth Rate: Fast
Soil: Fertile, well drained
Maintenance: Trim to shape and control growth.
Comments: Superb, trouble-free landscape plant for use as a specimen or hedge. One of the best green around. Small flowers attract bees.

Spring Bouquet Viburnum
(*Viburnum tinus* 'Compactum,'
  V. tinus 'Spring Bouquet')
Birds
Evergreen
Height: 4 feet
Spread: 4 feet
Bloom Time: Spring
Bloom Color: Whitish pink
Growth Rate: Moderate to fast
Soil: Fertile, adaptable

Maintenance: Trim to shape. Apply a general-purpose fertilizer in late winter.
Comments: Dense dark green foliage covered with masses of whitish pink blossoms in spring. Good as a foundation or hedge plant. No pest problems. Easy care.

CHAPTER 10

Vines and Climbers

VINES AND climbers are among our most serviceable plants. They can go places that are inaccessible to other plants—up, under and over, in and out, and around. They are good for defining spaces or concealing or softening the appearance of buildings or service areas. Vines can turn a chain-link fence into a hanging basket. A few vines noted for their tenacious growth—the ivies and Asian jasmine—serve well as ground covers in areas where there is little or no foot traffic. Many vines have spectacular blossoms and/or colorful fruit. They may be evergreen or deciduous. Most vines and climbers tend to be vigorous growers.

There are three basic ways vines climb:

- Twining. Vines that spiral around require the support of an open lattice, trellis, or wire fencing. Star jasmine is a twiner.
- Attaching by tendrils. These vines also require support or will quickly attach themselves to nearby plants. Passionflowers have tendrils.
- Clinging to a surface with small disks or rootlike projections. Caution: Clingers may weaken the mortar in stone and brick walls and/ or leave ugly marks when removed. Creeping fig and English ivy are clingers.

Consider the way vines support themselves before you make your purchase.

Planting Vines and Climbers

When planting, place the vine at least 1 foot from the surface of its intended support structure. But remember that soil near building foundations, a popular location for vines and other climbers, often is poor and compacted and requires enrichment with organic matter as well as watering. As with any plant, make a generous-sized hole to allow roots to spread freely.

Maintenance

Vines seldom need fertilizer. In fact, keeping vines neat and their growth in check is the most important maintenance chore for these plants. Gardeners often neglect pruning their vines until the situation is out of control. Many vines will survive severe treatment with the pruning shears, but the gardener who regularly removes suckers, dead

sections, and wayward stems will be rewarded with an orderly appearance. Keep vines out of the trees. As romantic as it might look, vines growing in trees can make the trees susceptible to insect infestations, top heavy, and vulnerable in high winds. Because old growth once separated from its support will not reattach itself, clinging vines that have fallen from their supports need to be cut back, and the emergent, new growth should be supported by ties or hooks until the vine is reestablished. Most vines, especially those that produce flowers, should be pruned back when they are dormant. A good guideline is to prune out one-third of the old growth.

Vines and Climbers for Central Texas

Butterfly Vine
(*Mascagnia macroptera*)
Deciduous
Height: 10–20 feet
Spread: 12 feet
Flower: Yellow paddle-shaped
blooms in spring and fall
Soil: Adaptable

Maintenance: Needs support.
Prune to 2 feet in late winter to
reinvigorate.

Comments: The butterfly-shaped
seed pods that turn brown
as they mature give this fast-
growing, very heat-tolerant
vine its name. While regarded
as fairly drought tolerant, it
responds well to occasional
water. Being pest-free and having unusual yellow blossoms
make this a desirable choice.

Carolina Jessamine
(*Gelsemium sempervirens*)
Evergreen
Height: 15–20 feet
Spread: 12 feet
Flower: Yellow, January to March
Soil: Adaptable
Maintenance: Prune to keep
    vigorous.

Comments: The native range of
    South Carolina's state flower
    extends to East Texas, and it
    does just fine in Central Texas
    if its soil is not allowed to dry
    out. Its leaves are small and
    delicate. Its appearance ben-
    efits from being trained. All
    parts are poisonous.

Climbing Fig, Creeping Fig
(*Ficus pumila*)
Evergreen
Height: 10–15 feet
Spread: 5 feet
Flower: None
Soil: Organically enriched
Maintenance: Medium to high, depending on how you want it to present. I once saw this vine espaliered on a limestone wall, and it took my breath away. It grows very fast and will require regular pruning or shearing to maintain a neat appearance.

Comments: Finely textured and very shade tolerant, the creeping fig is a versatile and elegant vine for covering stone or brick walls. It is not recommended for wooden fences. Harsh winters may cause this vine to die back, but it will return from roots the following spring.

Coral Honeysuckle
(*Lonicera sempervirens*)
Evergreen
Height: 10–12 feet
Spread: 5–8 feet
Flower: Scarlet or orange, March
   to May
Soil: Adaptable
Maintenance: Minimal, may be
   trimmed to shape

Comments: The vivid color of this native vine more than makes up for its lack of scent. Hummingbirds are attracted to the 1–2-inch blossoms, and cardinals and purple finches are fond of its fruit. Although drought tolerant, it flourishes with a bit of water. It looks best given some support.

Coralvine, Queen's Wreath
(*Antigonon leptopus*)
Deciduous
Height: 8–10 feet
Spread: 3–4 feet
Flower: Pink to white in mid-
   summer to early fall
Soil: Well drained
Maintenance: None

Comments: Known in Mexico as the "chain-of-love vine," this romantic-looking beauty comes into its own just as many others are withering in our midsummer heat. It grows fast and will cover its support rapidly. Be sure to give this one a nice display. It will die back after a frost but usually returns from the roots.

Crossvine
(*Bignonia capreolata*)
Semi-evergreen
Height: 35–50 feet
Spread: 6–9 feet
Flower: Sumptuous orange-red
    trumpetlike blossoms in early
    spring
Soil: Well-drained

Maintenance: Prune to control
    growth.
Comments: For best flowers,
    grow in full sun. An aggressive
    grower, the crossvine should
    be trained to a fence or arbor.
    No insect or disease problems.
    Look for cultivars 'Tangerine
    Beauty,' 'Jekyll,' and 'Shalimar
    Red.'

Purple Passionflower

(*Passiflora incarnata*)
Semi-evergreen
Height: 6–8 feet
Spread: 3–40 feet
Flower: Showy white with purple crown in summer
Soil: Well drained
Maintenance: May be invasive from the roots

Comments: This is a must-have butterfly garden plant. It is an aggressive grower. What really makes passionflowers so appealing is that they are magnets for the gulf fritillary butterfly. And if zebra longwings are in the vicinity, they, too, will come. Passionflowers are larval plants, so expect to see lots of caterpillars and chewed leaves. Established plants have no trouble recovering from the feasting caterpillars.

Star Jasmine
(*Trachelospermum jasminoides*)
Evergreen
Height: 20 feet
Spread: 1–2 feet
Flower: Fragrant, white petaled
   in spring
Soil: Organically enriched
Maintenance: Prune to control.

Comments: A staple in southern gardens so long that it is often affectionately called Confederate jasmine. This vine's dark, shiny, evergreen leaves provide an excellent background for clusters of fragrant white flowers. Growing well in a variety of conditions, it is better as a climber than ground cover. Does well planted in containers.

Trumpetvine, Trumpetcreeper
(*Campsis radicans*)
Deciduous
Height: 36–72 feet
Spread: 12 feet
Flower: Red, orange trumpet-
   shaped blooms June through
   September
Soil: Adaptable

Maintenance: This very aggressive clinger needs lots of room
   and strong support. It flowers
   on new growth, so late-winter
   pruning is ideal.
Comments: Blooms best in full
   sun. A stunning plant but
   needs to be kept in check.

Virginia Creeper
(*Parthenocissus quinquefolia*)
Deciduous
Height: 12–36 feet
Spread: 12 feet
Flower: Inconspicuous in May to
    June
Soil: Adaptable
Maintenance: Little or none
Comments: Attractive leaves turn
scarlet in autumn. Virginia creeper is a welcome addition for an area notably lacking red fall color. It does equally well clinging to trees, walls, and fences or trailing on the ground, and it tolerates full sun to partial shade. Caution: The insecticide Sevin will defoliate the vine. Has poisonous berries.

Clematis (Clematis *spp.*)

Two native species of this delicately branching genus bear beautiful, conspicuous flowers that make them desirable for home garden cultivation, especially in native plant collections. Both bloom best in moist conditions, but they have good heat and drought tolerance and are reported to be moderately deer resistant.

Leatherleaf Clematis

(*Clematis pitcheri*)

Deciduous

Height: 6–12 feet

Spread: 8 feet

Flower: Long-lasting purple bell-shaped flowers June through August

Soil: Moist, well drained, limestone based

Maintenance: Flowers are most visible if given support of a trellis or fence.

Comments: This delicate-looking vine needs to be given space of its own to be appreciated. Large, conspicuous seeds are a source of food for birds.

Scarlet Clematis
(*Clematis texensis* Buckl.)
Deciduous
Height: 6–12 feet
Spread: 8 feet
Flower: Red to deep pink bell-shaped flowers March through July

Soil: Moist, well drained, limestone based
Maintenance: Flowers are most visible if given support of a trellis or fence.
Comments: Cold and heat tolerant, this clematis blooms best with a half day of sunshine.

Flowers

Flowers are the faces of the garden. They demand our attention and compel us to admire their colors and shapes and marvel at their forms. With planning, Central Texas gardeners can have flowers in the garden year-round. Spring and early summer are our best months for flowers; wildflowers and spring-blooming bulbs abound. In summer the heat lovers, lantana and zinnias, see us through until the new flush of late summer and fall color (asters, Mexican marigold mint, and oxblood lilies) bursts on the scene. The winter months bring us bright and cheerful cool-season annuals and ornamental kale and cabbage.

The now familiar and prudent gardener's litany (careful selection, the right plant in the right location, good soil preparation, and appropriate maintenance) is as applicable here as for any other kind of gardening. Gardeners who do their homework and learn everything they need to know about the flowers they plant, no doubt, will have the most successful flower gardens. This is good. But flowers are lots of fun, and there are so many different kinds to delight and surprise us. They are, for the most part, inexpensive and do not require the hard, heavy manual labor required for tree and shrub planting. The flower bed is the place in the garden to give way to a little impulse and have fun. Annuals will be gone in a year anyway.

Planning the Flower Bed

The following guidelines will help you plan your flower garden.

Group according to needs. Gardening chores will be easier and plants will do better if you group plants with similar exposure, watering, and fertilizer needs. Be sure to note on your plan spacing requirements and flower heights. Taller flowers should not be relegated automatically to the back row, but they should not be allowed to shade smaller plants or to block your view of them. As obvious as this sounds, it is incredibly easy to get distracted and lose track of important details.

Consider color and light. Using crayons or colored markers when making the plan will help you envision the overall effect of your color scheme. Keep in mind that as spring advances to summer, the flower colors grow more intense. Spring brings us soft blues and pinks of larkspur, the white of sweet alyssum, and the cool purple and pale yellow of iris. In summer we enjoy the hot oranges, reds, and vivid yellows of zinnias and sunflowers. In late summer and autumn a dominant golden glow highlights the soft purple of Mexican sage and the mauve of the sedum 'Autumn Joy.' A white garden, enchanting in the low-light conditions of evening and on cloudy days, is even better in moonlight. The gray foliage of dusty miller brings out the best of all colors planted near it. Whether you prefer the excitement of a riot of color or the peacefulness

of color harmony, sometimes it is best to have the surprises show up on paper first.

Consider location. Many flowers bloom best if they receive six to eight hours of sun. Others such as impatiens and caladiums prefer shade. The kinder, cooler morning sun is preferable for flowers that require full sun when grown at higher elevation or more northern latitudes. This is especially true for shallow-rooted plants. Try to place your beds so that they do not interfere with your other garden uses. Avoid creating small, isolated beds scattered about the yard. These are not only a maintenance nightmare, but as Frederick Law Olmsted observed, "Make no small plans, they have not the strength to move men's minds." Olmsted, of course, was probably thinking of his greatest design, Central Park, but the point is well taken for the home landscape as well.

Think maintenance. Consider the amount of time and care you wish to devote to garden work. Routine flower bed chores include watering, mulching, weeding, and fertilizing. Perennials demand more work and attention in the initial preparation, but once established, they can go on for years with a bit of fertilizer and occasional dividing when they become too crowded or have stopped flowering. Some taller perennials may require staking for support. Annuals must be replanted each year and watered and fertilized more frequently. Some bulbs, such as caladiums, should be lifted up and stored if they are to be used the following year. Many gardeners find it easier to simply consider such bulbs as annuals and start over with a new set next season. Flowers grown in containers provide color for small areas at a reduced workload. A trowel will do the job of the garden spade; a watering can replaces miles of hose.

Consider the impact. Finally, a flower garden with little in bloom does not give much pleasure. Avoid dots of color by planting enough flowers. Many flowers, particularly annuals, look great in masses; others can hold their own in smaller groups of three to five. Choose your flowers to provide a succession of color throughout the year. A mix of annuals and perennials, along with dwarf shrubs and accent plants, provides diversity of texture, color, size, foliage, an fragrance.

Annuals

Because their lives span only one season, annuals tirelessly produce a profusion of blossoms in an effort to make seed and ensure another generation. Annuals may be grown from seed or purchased as bedding plants from garden centers. Seed is most economical, but today most of us opt for the convenience, ease, and instant color of inexpensive six-packs or 4-inch pots.

If you are creating a flower bed for the first time, prepare the soil a couple of weeks before planting. Loosen soil, remove any weeds and rocks, and add lots of compost (3 to 4 inches, at least). Just before you plant, cultivate again, add more organic matter, and work in the proper amount of fertilizer in a 1-2-1 ratio. (See chapter 2 for more detailed instructions for creating a bed and information on fertilizers.)

Preparing to Plant. Transplant seedlings from flats or container-started plants into holes large enough for the entire root system to extend downward. If the plant is root-bound—and frequently plants are—rough up the root ball, or even butterfly it with a sharp knife, to loosen the soil and free some roots to encourage them to grow out. Water well, and gently firm the soil around the plants. Apply 2 inches of organic mulch, such as compost or shredded bark, leaving a space of 2 or 3 inches between the mulch and the plant. Water again after you have applied the mulch. You may want to shade the tender seedlings for a day or two to reduce heat stress.

Thinning. If you have started your annuals from seed, you will need to thin the seedlings when they have put out their first pair of true leaves to ensure they receive the right amount of light, space, and water to thrive. Follow the directions on the seed packet for recommended spacing.

Fertilizing. For a continuous display of healthy-looking blooms, fertilize with a complete fertilizer two to three times during the season. This is especially important if you apply an organic mulch, which will use some of the nitrogen as it decomposes.

Watering. When the soil is dry, water to a depth of 1 or 2 inches. Since many annuals are susceptible to mildew, watering by soaker hose is preferable to using an overhead sprinkler.

Mulching. Use an organic mulch to conserve water, moderate temperature, and prevent soil from crusting and weeds from germinating.

Deadheading. Removing, or deadheading, spent flowers on annuals prevents the plant from using energy to make seed and prolongs bloom time. It also improves the garden's appearance.

Warm-Season Bloomers

Coleus
(*Coleus* spp.)
Height: 2–3 feet
Spread: 1–3 feet
Foliage Color: Burgundy, plum

Comments: In 1995, Texas A&M horticulturists introduced the first sun-loving coleus well suited to all areas of Texas. Highly resistant to disease and insects, these coleus plants keep their rich, vivid, colorful leaves all season long. Adaptable to many soils, they ask only for good drainage. This superior bedding plant is also great in containers. Look for Texas Superstars SuperSun 'Burgundy Sun' and SuperSun 'Plum Parfait.'

Cosmos
(*Cosmos sulphureus*)
Height: 2–5 feet
Spread: 1–3 feet
Bloom Color: Yellow, orange
Comments: The yellow cosmos
are easy to start from seed and
require minimum care. They
are Texas tough and grow in
harsh conditions. Pampering
will result in lanky plants

with excessive foliage.
C. bipinnatus are pink, white,
purple, and red with delicate,
lacy foliage and grow to 4 feet.
A delightful old-fashioned
garden favorite, it is easy to
start from seed or is readily
available in single and double
cultivars as transplants. Unlike *C. sulphureus,* it is prone
to mildew in our humidity. It
is, however, the quintessential
cottage garden flower. Cosmos
does best in the early part of
the season, fading in the worst
of the heat and humidity.

Dusty Miller
(*Centaurea cineraria*)
Height: 6–12 inches
Spread: 6–12 inches
Foliage Color: Gray

Comments: Occasionally producing small yellow flowers, dusty miller is prized for its gray fernlike foliage. It makes everything planted near it look great, whether in a container or flower bed.

Globe Amaranth
(*Gomphrena globosa*)
Height: 1–2 feet
Spread: ½–1 foot
Bloom Color: Magenta, straw-
  berry, lilac, white

Comments: A cheerful addition
  to any flower garden, the globe
  amaranth is easy to grow and
  quite drought tolerant once
  established. It will bloom from
  summer until frost and will
  likely, but not reliably, reseed.
  Extremely heat tolerant. Soil
  should be well drained. Grow
  in masses for best visual
  impact.

Impatiens
(*Impatiens walleriana*)
Height: 6–18 inches
Spread: 10–18 inches
Bloom Color: Red, rose, purple, lilac, pink, orange, white

Comments: What would we do without impatiens! They are our number-one bedding plant for shade. Blooming profusely from spring till frost, they brighten dark areas and enliven container gardens. Pinch back to encourage branching or control growth.

Madagascar Periwinkle
(*Catharanthus roseus*)
Height: 6–12 inches
Spread: 6–18 inches
Bloom Color: Pink, mauve, white

Comments: The profuse bloomer
has excellent heat tolerance
for our summers. Do not overwater once established. Looks
good all season long. For best
effect, plant in masses.

Mari-mum
(*Tagetes erecta* 'Antiqua')
Height: 14–16 inches
Spread: 12–15 inches
Bloom Color: Yellow

Comments: Plant this Texas Superstar (cross between a marigold and chrysanthemum) in full sun and well-drained soil, and you're set for summer and fall color in your garden. Has good resistance to spider mites. 'Voyager Yellow' grows to 14–16 inches. Dwarf varieties (8–10 inches) include 'Discovery Yellow' and 'Discovery Orange.' After planting, water daily until established, then every five to seven days.

Mexican Sunflower
(*Tithonia rotundifolia*)
Height: 4–6 feet
Spread: 3–4 feet
Bloom Color: Orange

Comments: So good in hot weather, and such a rich orange! A good-sized plant with handsome foliage and a profusion of large blossoms makes this a standout in a medium to large space. Plant in well-drained soil that is not too fertile. Deadhead to prolong flowering. Makes a nice cut flower.

Pentas

(*Pentas lanceolata*)

Height: 1–2 feet, dwarf varieties to 10 inches

Spread: 1–2 feet, dwarf varieties to 10 inches

Bloom Color: Red, magenta, lilac, pink

Comments: Handsome dark green foliage, a neat growth habit, and clusters of starlike flowers make this butterfly attractor a desirable denizen of the garden.

Petunia
(*Petunia* spp.)
Height: 18–20 inches
Spread: 12–30 inches
Bloom Color: Pink, mauve. 'Tidal
   Wave Silver' is white with a
   lilac blush.

Comments: There are dozens of
   petunia cultivars to choose
   from, so why not pick Texas
   Superstars like 'Laura Bush,'
   'Tidal Wave Cherry,' Tidal
   Wave Silver,' and 'VIP'? They
   all thrive in our challenging
   heat and humidity. Slow-
   release fertilizer applied one
   week after planting is recommended. Petunia blossoms
   may wilt and close when they
   come in contact with water.
   For that reason it is best to water with a wand.

Portulaca, Moss Rose
(*Portulaca grandiflora*)
Height: 6–10 inches
Spread: 6–12 inches
Bloom Color: Red, rose, yellow, orange, white

Comments: One tough cookie that grows well in poor to average soil as long as it is well drained. Blooms its heart out till frost. May spread to 12 inches and naturalize. Succulent-like leaves. Looks great trailing from hanging baskets and limestone walls.

Tall Verbena
(*Verbena bonariensis*)
Height: 3–5 feet
Spread: 1–3 feet
Bloom Color: Lavender, violet

Comments: A short-lived, tender perennial that is best grown as an annual in Central Texas. It attracts many species and is a must-have for anyone interested in butterflies and hummingbirds. Tall with an open habit, it will not shade or crowd other plants. Reseeds easily but is never a pest.

Wax Begonia
(*Begonia semperflorens*)
Height: 6–12 inches
Spread: 6 inches
Bloom Color: White, pink, red

Comments: Begonias like organically enriched soil but do poorly in heavy clay. They are excellent in borders and mass plantings. Their attractive bronze foliage makes them ideal container garden plants.

Zinnia

(*Zinnia* spp.)

Height: 6–48 inches

Spread: 6–18 inches

Bloom Color: Many colors, but not blue

Comments: There is no flower easier to grow from seed. There are single and double blossoms, short or tall, single-color and multicolor zinnias. They are low-maintenance plants but do best in evenly moist and well-drained soil. Look for disease-resistant varieties, and be sure they have good air circulation to prevent powdery mildew and other fungal diseases. My favorites are the old-fashioned 'Cut and Come Again' and **Narrow-leaf Zinnia** (*Z. angustifolia*), a short, small-flowered, narrow-leaved zinnia that resembles the wildflower blackfoot daisy. It is well suited to container gardens as well as flower beds. It is available in white or orange.

Cool-Season Bloomers

Calendula
(*Calendula officinalis*)
Height: 1–2 feet
Spread: 1–2 feet
Bloom Color: Yellow, bright gold

Comments: Nice, large, mum-like blossom for cool weather. Does best in well-drained soil. Deadheading will promote more flowers. Good in containers.

California Poppy
(*Eschscholzia californica*)
Height: 1–2 feet
Spread: 1–2 feet
Bloom Color: Orange, orange-
yellow

Comments: Soil needs to be well
drained with a little grit and
not too fertile. May reseed
but not reliably. Available in
transplants, but because of its
long taproot, it is better to start
from seed.

Cyclamen
(*Cyclamen persicum*)
Height: 6–10 inches
Spread: 6–10 inches
Bloom Color: Red, pink, violet,
    lavender, white

Comments: For best results grow
    in fertile, well-drained soil.
    Tolerates shade very well.
    Lovely variegated foliage and
    exotic blossoms add color and
    interest in late fall through ear-
    ly spring. Excellent container
    plant.

Flowering Kale, Ornamental Cabbage

(*Brassica oleracea*)

Height: 1–2 feet

Spread: 1–2 feet

Foliage Color: Gray-green with hues of purple, red, and lavender

Comments: Grown together, flowering kale and ornamental cabbage make a handsome combination, providing lovely color throughout the fall and winter. Likes organically rich soil and even moisture. Soil should be well drained. Remove any flower stalks that develop.

Larkspur
(*Consolida ambigua*)
Height: 3 feet
Spread: 1–1½ feet
Bloom Color: Blue, purple, pink
 with white

Comments: Larkspur have good height and bloom all spring long. They require well-drained soil. Easily grown from seed, transplants are also available. **Bunny Bloom Larkspur** (*C. ambigua* 'Bunny Bloom') is a Texas Superstar worth asking for.

Pansy
(*Viola* × *wittrockiana*)
Height: 6–10 inches
Spread: 9–12 inches
Bloom Color: Many colors, in-
cluding bicolors

Comments: Likes moist, organically enriched, well-drained
soil. Presenting a big display,
jumbo-sized pansies are very
popular at the garden center,
but the smaller-bloomed varieties are less likely to flop
or fold. Superb container
and bedding flowers for cool
weather. Pansies will fade
away with the onset of hot
weather in April or May.

Poppy
(*Papaver* spp.)
Height: 2–4 feet
Spread: 1–2 feet
Bloom Color: Shades of red, pink, orange, white

Comments: Needs well-drained soil. Looks best in masses. Tall and vibrantly colored, these annuals make a big statement and reseed readily. Many varieties available, including doubles. Try Iceland and Corn/ Flanders poppies for an explosion of color in the spring garden.

Snapdragon
(*Antirrhinum majus*)
Height: 1–3 feet
Spread: ½–1 foot
Bloom Color: Pink, yellow,
   white, red, peach, orange

Comments: This old-fashioned
   favorite still gives some of the
   best garden color in the cool
   season. Many cultivars are
   available, including dwarf and
   fungal-resistant strains. Will
   bloom as long as temperatures
   are above freezing. Likes well-
   drained and organically enriched soil. Plant in masses.

Sweet Alyssum
(*Lobularia maritima*)
Height: 4–6 inches
Spread: 6–14 inches
Bloom Color: White, rose, pink

Comments: A spreading habit and tight clusters of sweetly fragrant flowers. Good in containers and in a front location in borders and flower beds. Performs best when planted in organically enriched soil.

Perennials

A seemingly infinite variety and low maintenance leave little reason to wonder why perennials are so popular. Perennials, too, hold one's interest throughout the season as they emerge, develop, and finally bloom. Because they are around for a while, perennials require more careful planning and bed preparation than annuals, where a mistake just need not be repeated next year. Fertilizer can be applied periodically to restore nutrients, but improving soil is more difficult once a flower bed has been established. Clay soils tend to get compacted over the years, denying root systems proper air circulation. If poor drainage is likely to be a problem because of clay soil and flat terrain, consider planting your perennials in raised beds. Very sandy soils drain too rapidly for many moisture-loving perennials.

Soil Preparation. Prepare your soil well in advance of planting. Begin by incorporating a 4- to 6-inch layer of compost or well-rotted manure. The bed should be dug deeply (12 to 15 inches, ideally). Work a light application of low-nitrogen fertilizer into the soil.

Planting. Although some perennials can be started from seed, many varieties that have been developed to produce very colorful, ruffled, or extra large blossoms propagate asexually only. For these, it makes sense to purchase container-grown or dormant bare-root plants at nurseries or through mail-order suppliers.

Container-raised plants can be planted almost any time but midsummer. Fall is the optimum time to plant bare-root perennials. When you plant, the hole

LIFE SPANS OF SELECTED PERENNIALS

Long-Lived Perennials	Short-Lived Perennials
Balloon flower	Blackberry lily
Black-eyed Susan	Columbine
Daylily	Coreopsis
Giant coneflower	Dianthus
Mexican marigold mint	Pincushion flower

The dictionary definition of perennial includes the terms "enduring," "perpetual," and "everlasting." In fact, not all our perennials adhere to that description. There are long-lived perennials that can go on for decades and short-lived perennials that begin to fade in three to five years. Short-lived perennials tend to propagate by seed as well as by other vegetative means such as sending out runners or developing bulbs.

moisture, hold down weeds, and moderate soil temperature. Water again after mulching.

Maintenance. In addition to continuing good watering, fertilizing, weeding, and mulching practices, you will need to divide your perennials from time to time to keep them vigorous and blooming year after year. Rule of thumb is to divide early-blooming perennials in fall and late bloomers in early spring. Avoid dividing in the heat of summer.

Division. To divide, dig and lift out the plant or clump of plants with a spading fork. This may be a formidable task if the plant has been in the same location undivided for several years. If the plant has a small root system, gently pry apart the plants to separate. Washing the soil off the plants with the hose will make this easier to do. You may need to separate heavier, matted clumps by driving two forks back to back into the root ball and easing them apart. Finally, there may be times when you have to use a hatchet or pruning saw to cut through the plant mass. Trim off any damaged or dead roots. Work some compost into the soil before replanting. When dividing bearded iris, cut the rhizomes apart with pruning

must be large enough (at least twice the diameter of the plant container) to allow the roots to spread down and out. Container-grown plants should be planted at the same depth as they were in their pots. It is easy to determine how deeply to plant dormant plants by finding the soil mark from the previous season's growth. If the plants will be tall and are likely to need support, now is the time to insert support stakes to avoid disturbing the root systems later in the season.

After planting, water thoroughly, and gently firm the soil to make certain there are no air pockets. Mulch to conserve shears or a sharp knife along the visible line that marks the rhizome segments. Discard the old center and any rhizome pieces that are mushy, smelly, or rid- dled with insect holes. Dust the raw rhizome ends with dusting sulfur to prevent rot. Replant, leaving just the top surface of the rhizome exposed.

Perennials Checklist

Artemisia
(*Artemisia* ×'Powis Castle')
Height: 2–3 feet
Spread: 1–2 feet
Foliage Color: Yellow
Bloom Time: Late summer to fall

Comments: Prized most for its feathery gray foliage that works well with so many other plants.

Balloon Flower
(*Platycodon grandiflorus*)
Height: 2–4 feet
Spread: 1–1½ feet
Bloom Color: Purplish blue
Bloom Time: Late spring to
    summer

Comments: Dies back to the
    ground completely and emerg-
    es later than other perennials,
    so it's a good idea to mark its
    place in the garden—the plant
    is too lovely to accidentally
    dig up. An exquisite old gar-
    den standard, it's nice to see
    it gaining popularity at local
    garden centers again.

Black-eyed Susan
(*Rudbeckia fulgida*)
Birds
Height: 2–3 feet
Spread: 2–2½ feet
Bloom Color: Orange-gold, black
    center
Bloom Time: Late spring to fall

Comments: Named 1999 Perennial of the Year. Long blooming, pure color, and striking dark green foliage define this exceptionally handsome flower. Reseeds readily and propagates by roots. Suitable for Xeriscaping once established.

Blackfoot Daisy
(*Melampodium leucanthum*)
Height: 10–12 inches
Spread: 12–24 inches
Bloom Color: White with yellow
   center
Bloom Time: March to October

Comments: Does best in rocky, gravelly, limestone-based soils. Tolerates caliche, but good drainage is essential. Great in rock gardens. A superb native for the garden if you don't pamper it.

Columbine

(*Aquilega* spp.)
Height: 2 feet
Spread: 1–2 feet
Bloom Color: Yellow, multi-
 colored
Bloom Time: Early spring
Comments: Texas Superstar

'Texas Gold' is a lovely, large rocket-shaped flower with scalloped green leaves. Also look for the Hill Country native, *A. canadensis*. It is a smaller (8 inches) and more delicate plant with charming red-and-yellow flowers. There are many showy cultivars available at nurseries, but the more durable natives are preferred for Central Texas.

Copper Canyon Daisy
(*Tagetes lemmonii*)
Height: 4 feet
Spread: 4–5 feet
Bloom Color: Yellow
Bloom Time: Summer to fall

Comments: Extreme drought and deer resistance in addition to a massive profusion of blossoms spell success for the copper canyon daisy. Needs well-drained soil; tolerates caliche. Has pungent aroma.

Fall Aster
(*Symphyotrichum oblongifolium*)
Height: 2 feet
Spread: 1½–3 feet
Bloom Color: Purple, violet
Bloom Time: September to
November

Comments: This lovely purple flower with a yellow center bursts onto the scene just when we need to be refreshed. Much beloved by bees as well as butterflies. Various cultivars available at nurseries.

Four-nerve Daisy
(*Tetraneuris scaposa*)
Height: 1 foot
Spread: 1–2 feet
Bloom Color: Yellow
Bloom Time: March to October

Comments: Another excellent native for the garden, especially a rock garden. Nice companion plant for the blackfoot daisy. Requires excellent drainage. Has attractive foliage with a clumping growth habit.

Giant Coneflower
(*Rudbeckia maxima*)
Height: 3–6 feet
Spread: 2–3 feet
Bloom Color: Yellow petals sur-
  rounding large dark brown cone
Bloom Time: May to September

Comments: Its height and large
  gray leaves make the giant
  coneflower a bold addition to
  the garden. Will reseed. Cut
  back after blooming, and remove dead leaves at the base.

Lantana
(*Lantana* spp.)
Height: Varies greatly by species
Spread: Varies greatly by species
Bloom Color: Many colors
Bloom Time: Sporadically
   throughout the season
Comments: The lantanas are
   such a good choice for our
   area. We are lucky to have so
   many varieties—from the na-
   tive orange and gold **Texas**

Lantana (*L. urticoides*), pink
and cream **Desert Lantana** (*L.
achyranthifolia*) to the Texas
Superstars 'New Gold' and
Trailing Lantana (*L. montevi-
densis*). All are exceptionally
heat and drought tolerant. The
newer hybrids have showier
flowers and better shape, but
if I were planting lantana just
for butterflies, I would use the
common native varieties.

Mexican Marigold Mint
(*Tagetes lucida*)
Height: 1–2 feet
Spread: 1–2 feet
Bloom Color: Deep yellow

Comments: Upright, compact, with a tarragon-like aroma. Requires only good drainage. A heat-tolerant and care-free plant whose blooms refresh the garden just at the right time of year.

Pincushion Flower
(*Scabiosa columbaria* 'Butterfly Blue')
Height: 12–18 inches
Spread: 10–12 inches
Bloom Color: Lavender-blue
Bloom Time: April to frost; may take a respite during mid-summer

Comments: Named Perennial Plant of 2000. Nice size, interesting foliage, and a lovely blossom. Easy to grow in organically enriched and light soil. Deadhead to encourage new blooms.

Purple Coneflower

(*Echinacea purpurea*)

Height: 2–4 feet

Spread: 1½–2 feet

Bloom Color: Dark pink to rosy purple with golden center

Bloom Time: May to August

Comments: With a striking appearance, the purple coneflower is sturdy and undemanding and makes a great, long-lasting cut flower. Deadhead for a neat appearance, or enjoy watching the lesser goldfinches feast on the seed heads. A white cultivar, 'White Swan,' is lovely but less robust. Can be divided in spring or fall; also reseeds readily. Our native coneflower, *E. angustifolia,* is seldom seen commercially.

Skullcap
(*Scutellaria suffrutescens*)
Height: 6–8 inches
Spread: 12–24 inches
Bloom Color: Pink-rose
Bloom Time: May through No-
  vember

Comments: Compact plant with
  dense, mounding foliage
  makes it ideal for a ground
  cover. Great for rock gardens
  and borders. Loves heat and
  sun. Cutting back in early
  spring is about all the care it
  requires.

Spiderwort
(*Tradescantia* spp.)
Height: 1–2 feet
Spread: 1–2 feet
Bloom Color: Purple, blue, white
Bloom Time: Spring

Comments: This nice group of perennials brings vivid color and interesting texture to the garden. Foliage will disappear as summer heat sets in.

Square-bud Primrose, Sundrops
(*Calylophus berlandieri*)
Height: 1 foot
Spread: 1–2½ feet
Bloom Color: Lemon yellow
Bloom Time: Spring through fall

Comments: Compact and bushy, this primrose family member looks great in a rock garden or at the front edge of a flower bed. Extremely heat tolerant, it thrives in fast-draining soil. Profuse, 1-inch blossoms and fine, needlelike foliage. Trim lightly to shape. The **Western Primrose** (*C. hartwegii*) is even more drought tolerant.

Summer Phlox
(*Phlox paniculata* 'John Fanick')
Height: 4 feet
Spread: 1–2 feet
Bloom Color: Light pink
Bloom Time: Late spring to
   summer

Comments: The dense clusters of light pink flowers are very fragrant. Very heat and drought tolerant and resistant to powdery mildew. This variety is named for a San Antonio nurseryman. *P. paniculata* 'Victoria' is another desirable variety for Texas. It has a looser habit than 'John Fanick,' and its flowers are a darker pink.

Texas Betony
(*Stachys coccinea*)
Height: 1–3 feet
Spread: 1–2 feet
Bloom Color: Red
Bloom Time: Late spring through fall

Comments: This West Texas native is a good bloomer in shade and is highly deer resistant, a winning combination for Texas gardeners. It prefers moist, well-drained soil.

Tropical Milkweed

(*Asclepias curassavica*)

Height: 3–5 feet

Spread: 2–3 feet

Bloom Color: Orange and red, yellow

Bloom Time: Late spring through fall

Comments: Best monarch butterfly magnet. Dies back in a freeze but will return. Also reseeds easily. Most milkweeds, including natives, *A. tuberosa* and *A. asperula,* are superb butterfly plants, but I find the tropical easier to grow in a regular garden environment.

Salvias

Texans love salvias, and salvias love Texas. We have so many to choose from: red, blue, yellow; short, tall; skinny or bushy; salvias for sun, others for shade. The selected five varieties do well here with little care. New varieties seem to arrive at garden stores every year. Enjoy and explore.

Autumn Sage
(*Salvia greggii*)
Height: 3 feet
Spread: 3 feet
Bloom Color: Many colors
Bloom Time: Spring through fall
Comments: Very adaptable to various soil types. Originally available only in red, but there are now many hybrids in colors including yellow, salmon, fuchsia, and purple. Cut back by one-third twice each season to keep shape and control growth.

Brazilian Sage
(*Salvia guaranitica*)
Height: 3–4 feet
Spread: 3 feet
Bloom Color: Electric royal blue
Bloom Time: Spring through fall

Comments: This has to be one of the best blues in the garden! And if that isn't good enough, try the 'Black and Blue' cultivar that is even more striking. The ruby-throat hummingbird adores this plant. Brazilian sage spreads easily by roots; the 'Black and Blue' does not.

Indigo Spires
(*Salvia* × 'Indigo Spires')
Height: 3–5 feet
Spread: 3–6 feet
Bloom Color: Purplish blue
Bloom Time: Early summer
   through fall

Comments: One of the most
   popular garden salvias, indigo
   spires thrives on neglect and
   withstands humidity better
   than *S. farinacea*. Dies back
   after frost; reliably returns.

Mexican Bush Sage
(*Salvia leucantha*)
Height: 2–6 feet
Spread: 2–4 feet
Bloom Color: Soft purple
Bloom Time: Summer through
  fall

Comments: Looks best if sheared back in late winter. It spreads widely, so give it room to grow. Its silver foliage and velvety flowers are a stunning combination.

Scarlet Sage, Texas Sage
(*Salvia coccinea*)
Height: 1–2 feet
Spread: 1–2 feet
Bloom Color: Fire red
Bloom Time: Summer through
    fall

Comments: This native sage does
    best in well-drained soils. Its
    bold, vivid color makes a stun-
    ning statement when planted
    in masses. This is an excellent
    low-maintenance plant.

Verbenas

There are many verbenas for Central Texas. Some are annual; others, perennial. Both cultivars and natives are available. They are useful in a range of settings—rock gardens, borders, and containers. Many are good butterfly and hummingbird attractors. See listings for other verbenas in "Annuals" and "Wildflowers" sections of this chapter.

Garden Verbena
(*Verbena × hybrida*)
Height: Varies by species
Spread: Varies by species
Bloom Color: Many colors, mostly in the blue, pink, purple range
Bloom Time: Spring through fall
Comments: A willingness to go on blooming through thick or thin, good colors, a pleasing shape, and handsome foliage make this a deservingly popular plant.

Bulbs and Related Plants

Be they bulb, tuber, corm, or rhizome, they all begin as underground stems containing nutrients necessary to create and nurture a plant. Generally speaking, bulbs do best when grown in soils that drain well. Many are drought tolerant. Some bulbs last a year; others are long lived. Most of the early spring bloomers go dormant in summer, and summer-blooming bulbs, often of tropical origin, are dormant in winter. Indeed, one of the most bothersome aspects about bulbs is simply remembering where you planted them from one season to the next. It helps to devise some system (an outline of stones or cord of durable material) to mark their location so you do not plant over or through them while they lie dormant.

When preparing beds for bulbs, cultivate to a minimum depth of 6 to 12 inches. Dig in a good amount of compost to make a bottom layer in which the roots can spread. At this time, work in a high-phosphate fertilizer such as superphosphate or bone meal to ensure good root development. A good rule of thumb for planting is that bulbs are planted at a depth roughly three times their diameter. In heavy soils, they can be planted less deeply. In general, bulbs should be planted with the broader base at the bottom and tip pointing up. Most spring-blooming bulbs are planted from mid-October through December. Cannas and caladiums are planted in spring, after the soil has warmed. Water thoroughly after planting, and mulch (bearded iris is the exception). If the winter is a dry one, do not forget to water the beds.

After their flowers have faded, the bulbs will benefit from an application of 5-10-5 fertilizer. Do not remove the foliage, which is producing nourishment for the next season's growth, until it has yellowed and dried. Fertilize again in the fall and once more when the first leaves poke through the soil. Some bulbs should be replaced every year, and others may be left in the ground. Caladiums will perform better if they are taken up, properly stored, and replanted the next season. Remove any residual soil, and store dry bulbs in a paper bag or unsealed box filled with dry peat moss or vermiculite in a cool, dark location. Do not store in the refrigerator or anywhere the humidity is high. Many gardeners prefer to start the next season with fresh bulbs rather than store the old ones.

Bulbs Checklist

Agapanthus
(*Agapanthus africanus*)
Height: 1–2 feet
Spread: 1–2 feet
Bloom Color: Blue, white
Bloom Time: Late spring through summer

Comments: With handsome strap leaves and tall flower stalks topped with round heads of multiple blossoms, the agapanthus has an imposing presence in the garden. It likes rich, fertile soil and is evergreen to 25°F. Many other agapanthus varieties, including the popular dwarf 'Peter Pan,' are available.

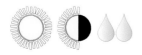

Anemone
(*Anemone coronaria*)
Height: 12–15 inches
Bloom Color: Red, blue, purple
Bloom Time: Spring

Comments: Soak tubers overnight before planting. Plant
with points down in humusy
soil with good drainage (tubers
will rot in heavy, wet clay).
Treat as an annual. Varieties
'Monarch de Caen,' 'St. Brig-
id,' and 'Blanda' will display
large, colorful flowers through
spring.

Bearded Iris
(*Iris germanica*)
Height: 12–36 inches
Bloom Color: Many colors
Bloom Time: Spring

Comments: Avoid fertilizer high in nitrogen. When planting, leave the top surface of the rhizome exposed. Large, colorful, and stately, bearded irises have a big presence in the garden. They perform very well in our heat but do not like heavy clay soil. Divide every two to three years to maintain their flowering vigor.

Butterfly Iris
(*Dietes bicolor*)
Height: 3 feet
Spread: 2 feet
Bloom Color: Creamy white pet-
als accented with yellow and
black
Bloom Time: Late spring to
summer

Comment: Evergreen swordlike
foliage and striking flower
form and color demand attention. Adaptable to different
soils. The related variety
Moraea grandiflora has a more
conventional irislike blossom
in white, purple, and yellow.

Caladium
(*Caladium* spp.)
Height: 12–15 inches
Foliage Color: Shades of pink, green, white
Bloom Time: Summer

Comments: Plant bulbs in May in rich soil. Large leaves brighten shady areas and give the landscape a tropical feel.

Canna
(*Canna* spp.)
Height: 3–5 feet
Bloom Color: Shades of yellow, orange, red
Bloom Time: Late spring to early summer

Comments: Big, bold leaves and exotic blossoms bring a tropical look to the garden. Fertilize with general garden fertilizer in late winter. Mulch to keep moist. Deadhead to maintain neat appearance. There are dwarf varieties (12–18 inches) for containers and aquatic cannas for water gardens.

Chinese Ground Orchid

(*Bletilla striata*)
Height: 18–24 inches
Bloom Color: Magenta, cream,
    white
Bloom Time: Spring

Comments: Loves moist, organi-
    cally enriched soil. Naturalizes
    slowly. Winter hardy but any
    newly emerging buds must
    be mulched in the event of a
    freeze or they will be nipped.
    Protect if a freeze is in the
    forecast so you do not miss the
    new season's flowers.

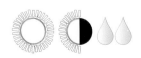

Crinum
(*Crinum* spp.)
Height: 3–4 feet
Bloom Color: Mostly white with
    purple and pink hues
Bloom Time: Spring, summer

Comments: Needs regular mois-
    ture and compost. This repeat
    bloomer has bold, large, fra-
    grant, lily-shaped blossoms.
    Crinum are very pest resistant
    and care-free. These big plants
    need lots of space. Many vari-
    eties are available.

Daylily
(*Hemerocallis* spp.)
Height: 6–24 inches
Bloom Color: Many colors; most
    common in the orange-yellow
    range
Bloom Time: Late spring to
summer

Comments: Tough and reliable.
    Divide tubers every few years
    to keep vigorous. Dwarf variet-
    ies available. 'Stella De Oro' is
    the longest-blooming variety.

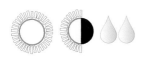

Grape Hyacinth
(*Muscari botryoides*)
Height: 6–10 inches
Bloom Color: Blue-purple
Bloom Time: Spring

Comments: One of the earliest spring bloomers. Has blue-purple flower spikes and grass-like leaves. Grape hyacinth looks best in mass plantings, naturalizes easily, and is care-free.

Narcissus
(*Narcissus* spp.)
Height: 10–15 inches
Bloom Color: Shades of yellow
and white
Bloom Time: Spring

Comments: Family includes daffodils and jonquils. Small-cup daffodils naturalize more readily in Central Texas than the large-cup varieties. Jonquils have small cups, are fragrant, and are quite successful in the South.

Oxblood Lily, Schoolhouse Lily
(*Rhodophiala bifida*)
Height: 1–2 feet
Bloom Color: Red, coral
Bloom Time: Fall

Comments: This old-fashioned favorite naturalizes well and tolerates a wide range of soil conditions, except boggy. Oxblood lilies are as durable as they are undemanding. Like its relative the amaryllis, it produces several flowers on each spike.

Rain Lily
(*Habranthus robustus*)
Height: 10–12 inches
Bloom Color: Pale pinkish white
Bloom Time: Intermittently late spring through summer

Comment: Take a hint from the species name. These large, hardy rain lilies multiply readily by seed and bulb production. You will be sharing them in no time. They bloom after a good rain but do not seem to respond to the hose. A delight!

Ranunculus
(*Ranunculus asiaticus*)
Height: 12–18 inches
Bloom Color: Many colors
Bloom Time: Spring

Comments: Treat as an annual. Pure colors and peony-like flowers make this early bloomer worth going the extra mile. Soak in water overnight before planting. Soil must be well drained. Look for Tecolote strain.

Snowflake
(*Leucojum aestivum*)
Height: 15–18 inches
Bloom Color: White
Bloom Time: Summer

Comments: Small bell-like flowers with deep green strap foliage. Very robust. Plant in masses. Naturalizes easily and prefers organically rich, moist soil. Unusual for most bulbs, the snowflake tolerates clay soil.

Spring Starflower
(*Ipheion uniflorum*)
Height: 4–8 inches
Bloom Color: White-violet and
   blue
Bloom Time: Early spring

Comments: Few bulbs say
   "spring" as readily as this
   small, delicate bulb. Likes
   well-drained soil and should
   be planted 2–3 inches deep.
   Does well in pots and may
   naturalize. These flowers are
   most effective when grown in
   masses, so buy at least ten to
   fifteen bulbs.

Toad Lily
(*Tricyrtis formosana*)
Height: 2–3 feet
Bloom Color: White speckled
   with deep purple spots
Bloom Time: Fall

Comments: A good bloomer in shady conditions. This plant's delightful and surprising blossoms never fail to bring a smile to one's face and are well worth the long wait until late summer. Handsome foliage lends interesting texture to the garden. Plants naturalize easily. They need organically enriched, moist soil.

Tulip

(*Tulipa* spp.)

Height: 1–2 feet

Bloom Color: Many colors

Bloom Time: Late winter through
early spring

Comments: There are more than
150 species of tulips to choose.
Many require a six- to eight-
week period in a paper bag in
the hydrator compartment of
the refrigerator prior to planting. I used to do this all the
time because tulips were syn-
onymous with spring. Even
with this kid-glove treatment,
the tulips were often gone after
a day or two if the temperature
got too high. Now for my tulip
fix, I limit myself to the *clu-
siana* species, which require
no chilling and frequently
naturalize under the right
conditions (no water in summer). Still, it's wisest to treat
all tulips as annuals in Central
Texas. Tulips like organically
rich and well-drained soil.

 **FYI: Bulbs**

PlantAnswers.com (http://www
.plantanswers.com/crinum.htm).
Retired Texas A&M University
professor Jerry M. Parsons offers
a good discussion of crinums
and other bulbs that do well in
Central Texas.

Wildflowers

It's hard not to be aware that Texas is a veritable flower basket. More than four thousand species of flowering plants have been identified in its varied regions, "where they smile in secret, looking over wasted

Damianita (Chrysactinia mexicana)

Barbara's Buttons (Marshallia caespitosa)

Foxglove (Penstemon cobea)

Coreopsis (Coreopsis spp.)

Blue-eyed Grasses (Sisyrinchium spp.)

Gayfeather (Liatris spp.*)*

Indian Blanket (Gaillardia pulchella)

Lemon Mint (Monarda citriodora)

Gulf Coast Penstemon (Penstemon tenuis)

Prairie Rain Lily (Cooperia pedunculata)

Wedelia (Zexmenia hispida)

Winecup (Callirhoe spp.)

Yellow Flax (Linum berlandieri)

lands."[1] Wildflower societies, the Texas State Highway Department, and commercial wildflower seed purveyors do their best to help Texans enjoy this renewable resource.

It wasn't too long ago that those of us who wanted to grow wildflowers were limited to collecting our own seed or seeking out the few seed houses that carried them. Now collections of wildflower mixes are found everywhere—from discount outlets to gift boutiques. Many, including the venerable Texas bluebonnet, are now container grown. Others have been tamed, hybridized, miniaturized, or colorized, further blurring the distinction between wildflower and "garden variety." In this book such wildflowers have been included in the checklists for annuals, perennials, and bulbs. Following is a partial list of other wildflowers that are worthy of consideration in the home landscape or garden but may be a little harder to find in garden centers that do not feature or carry many native plants. Many are easily grown from seed.

The Wildflower Meadow
Since many species of wildflowers look best when planted in

---

[1] Tennyson, "Song of the Lotus-Eaters,"

masses, the "meadow look" created by wildflowers interplanted
with native grasses can be an
excellent low-water-use alternative to the traditional turf lawn.
Before you choose this route and
broadcast bluebonnets across the
front yard, there are several factors to be considered. It is easy
to be seduced by the seemingly
indestructible appearance of
wildflowers, especially when we
see them growing through the
asphalt at the edges of roads or
in cracks in the sidewalks. For
many species, that crack in the
sidewalk is the perfect environment—and a difficult one for the
gardener to duplicate. Many a
blackfoot daisy or antelope horns

milkweed have been done in with
loving care and kindness. Rich,
fertile garden soil is not for all.
Also, while so beautiful and striking when in bloom, many wildflowers die after going to seed or
look like unwanted weeds a good
part of the year. The dazzling
display of spring flowers will be
short lived if the meadow or garden has not been sown or planted
for a succession of flowers.

When interplanting wildflowers with grass, use native grasses.
Their water needs are likely to be
similar to those of wildflowers,
and their growth habits are less
invasive than those of our common turf varieties, St. Augustinegrass and bermudagrass, which

will quickly outcompete any wildflower.

Knowing wildflower needs, strengths, and weaknesses is essential. A successful wildflower meadow requires planning, soil preparation, and time. Annuals will be up and blooming in a year, but the biennials and many perennials will not flower until the second year.

DIRECTIONS FOR PLANTING WILDFLOWER SEEDS

- Plant Texas wildflowers in the fall.
- Cultivate the soil surface to allow the seedlings to get a foothold.

- Spread each species separately if broadcasting several varieties. You will get a better distribution of plants. It is difficult to evenly spread a mix containing seeds of different sizes and weights, so it may be useful to mix very fine seeds with damp sand before spreading. Seed balls made of a clay and sand mix packed with seeds are occasionally available at stores featuring native plants.
- Cover seedlings lightly with soil, and firm gently. **Good contact with the soil is key to successful wildflower germination.**

Bluebonnet (Lupinus spp.)

- Water in well, and do not allow the soil to dry out completely for a couple of weeks. Many disappointing experiences with wildflowers are the result of scattered seed left to nature's course. Also, beware that wildflowers have a lower germination rate than that packet of marigold seeds you buy at the nursery.

Finally, a word about our state flower, the bluebonnet (*Lupinus* spp.). Texans seem to know at birth the bluebonnet is their state flower. But few probably know that not until 1971 did the state legislature deem all five native lupines, and any that might be discovered in the future, the state flower. Traditionally heralding spring with spikes of blue with white blossoms, the bluebonnet is now available in white, pink, and maroon. Bluebonnet seed should be planted in September (September 15 is the latest date to plant in Dallas; Thanksgiving in San Antonio). Transplants should be in the ground by the end of October in Dallas; by mid-February in San Antonio.

Texas Bluebonnets—Texas Pride (http://plantanswers.tamu.edu/flowers/bluebonnet/bluebonnetstory.html) recommends the following procedure to ensure a bumper crop of bluebonnets.

- Plant in full sun in soil that drains well and does not stay wet for long periods of time.
- Use transplants or chemically scarified seed.
- Barely cover seeds with soil; do not bury the crown of the transplants.
- Water seeds only on the day of planting and transplants only when the top inch of soil dries.
- Fertilize for more abundant blooms. No applications of fertilizer are required but are helpful.
- Interplant with pansies and other annuals for winter-long color.
- Don't overwater!

FYI: Wildflowers

Lady Bird Johnson Wildflower Center (http://www.wildflower.org/) is a superb resource for all kinds of native plant information. It has an excellent research library as well as superb fact

'Cornelia'

sheets available for a fee. Fact sheet topics include recommended species lists by geographic region, seed source lists, and wildlife and wildflower gardening.

Wildflowers in Bloom (http://aggie-horticulture.tamu.edu/wildseed/wildflowers.html) is a wonderful photo album of our most showy wildflowers. It contains range maps, photos of plants in various growth stages, and culture information.

Roses

Immortalized in poetry and celebrated in song, roses to many are the essence of flowers. Extolled in many cultures throughout history, the rose was named by Congress the national flower of the United States in 1986. Roses are native to Asia, Europe, and our own continent. There are climbing roses, trailing roses, shrub roses, tree roses, and miniature roses. Subject to endless hybridization in pursuit of the perfection of specific attributes, roses are now available for almost any taste and Central Texas garden. Volumes have been written on roses, and new roses are introduced continuously.

Old Roses. Pioneers brought roses to Texas to grace their gardens. As time went by, hybrid roses emphasizing large flowers

'Old Blush'

and spectacular color became
the fashion, and the charming
but less spectacular old roses
were overshadowed and often
ignored. In the late 1980s they
were "rediscovered" growing in
old cemeteries, at abandoned
homesteads, and along road-
sides. These hardy survivors
of past generations gained the
respect and attention of today's
rose growers for their unfussy
simplicity, fragrance, and toughness. Here were roses that, unlike many modern, demanding
hybrids, had come through neglect and our capricious climate
"smelling like a rose." Today
we are reaping the benefits of
those who set to work to cultivate these roses anew. New/old
vigorous varieties have taken
a well-earned place in the rose
section at many garden centers.
Old roses, an imprecise cate-

gory, fall into a variety of rose
classes. They can be teas, Chi-
nas, Noisettes, or Bourbons, for
instance. A good rule of thumb
for determining an old rose is
any rose that was introduced
seventy-five years ago or earlier.
The delicate pink 'Old Blush'
and climbing 'Old Blush,' the
fragrant, creamy yellow 'Céline
Forestier,' the petite pink 'The
Fairy,' and the prolific rose-
colored tea 'Mrs. B. R. Cant' are
popular old favorites.

Hybrid Teas. These roses are
what many of us "see" when we
think of a rose. The bush is generally upright in habit; a single,
pointed bud is produced on the
stem. Most blooms are usually
double and come in an extraordinary range of color. Well cared
for, they can be a spectacular and
sensuous experience. Although

'Sorbet'

'Strike It Rich'

fragrance often lost out to bloom size and color in many of the hybridization efforts, the pink 'Tiffany' and dark red 'Mirandy' are intoxicating exceptions. In our climate they bloom in spring and fall and intermittently in summer. They are hardy but require care to prevent disease and insect damage. Hybrid teas make wonderful cut flowers.

The old favorites, the red 'Chrysler Imperial' and yellow blend 'Peace,' are excellent examples of hybrid teas. Other desirable varieties are 'Alabama' (pink blend), 'Double Delight' (red blend), 'Helen Traubel' (pink blend), 'Honor' (white), and 'Pristine' (white).

Floribundas. Producing smaller flowers than the hybrid teas, the floribundas feature clusters of blossoms and color in the garden beginning in the spring and continuing through late fall, a longer time than hybrid tea roses. They

are also apt to be more hardy and disease resistant. They may be upright or spreading in habit.

'Angel Face' (mauve), 'Europeana' (dark red), 'Fire King' (orange-red), 'First Prize' (pink blend), 'Gene Boerner' (medium pink), 'Ginger' (orange-red), 'Handel' (red blend), 'Lawrence Pink Rosette' (pink), 'Sarabande' (orange-red), and 'Sorbet' (orange blend) are several varieties for Central Texas.

Grandifloras. A cross between the hybrid tea and the floribunda, the grandiflora is a tall, imposing bush that produces large blooms in clusters like floribunda and has the hardiness of the hybrid tea.

'Lady Banksia' (white)

'Mutabilis'

'Knockout'

Some recommended variet-
ies are 'Apricot Nectar' (apricot
blend), 'Aquarius' (pink blend),
'Camelot' (medium pink),
'Golden Girl' (medium yellow),
'Granada' (red blend), 'Montezu-
ma' (orange-red), 'Queen Elizabeth' (medium pink), and 'Strike
It Rich' (orange blend).

Polyanthas. Bountiful and
hardy, this class produces large
clusters of small flowers. Generally the bushes themselves are
smaller and more compact than
those of other classes, making
them particularly suitable for
small spaces and even containers. Some varieties are more fragrant than others. Good polyan-
tha varieties are 'Cécile Brünner'
(light pink) and the very fragrant
'Marie Pavie' (white).

Climbing Roses. Although
climbing roses have no special
climbing equipment, such as
tendrils or suction disks, they
vigorously produce long shoots
or canes that can be trained
over fences and trellises and
can make a perfect screen while
providing a profusion of blossoms. The flowers of today's
climbers can resemble those of
hybrid teas or floribundas. If
you have a small yard, bear in
mind that all climbers require
space, and some have a limited
blooming season. Attention to

pruning is essential to their
control.

The more popular are climbing 'Cécile Brünner' (light pink),
'Don Juan' (dark red), 'Golden
Showers' (medium yellow), the
tough 'Lady Banksia' (most often
seen in the thornless, yellow variety but also available in white,
which does have thorns and a
mild violet-like scent), 'Mermaid'
(creamy white), and 'New Dawn'
(light pink).

Mutabilis. This is an old China
rose introduced in 1894 and
named Earth-Kind Rose of the
Year in 2005 by Texas Cooperative Extension's Earth-Kind team.
With little care, it produces
masses of blossoms that open
gold, change to pink, and
finally turn crimson. It is a
repeat bloomer, grows in almost
any soil, and rarely requires a
pesticide. It will grow to 6 or 7
feet.

Planting Rosebushes

Site selection is key to successful roses. No amount of loving
care can compensate for an inadequate location. Roses need sun
and lots of it. Six to eight hours
daily will do nicely. And while
most roses, especially the modern hybrids, appreciate regular
watering, good drainage is

Black spot

essential. Because many rose varieties are prone to the fungal diseases black spot and mildew, roses should be given plenty of space for air circulation.

Planting. Bare-root roses arrive at garden centers from December through February. They should be planted immediately or covered with moist peat moss or soil until you can plant them properly. They will benefit from an overnight soak before planting. Container roses can be planted anytime, but spring and fall are preferable. Roses like slight acidity—a pH of 6.0 to 6.5—so chances are you will have to add bone meal or superphosphate as well as a large amount of humus

to the soil. Dig your hole about 12 inches deep and at least 1½–3 feet wide, depending on variety. Consider a raised bed if you have heavy clay soil or inadequate soil depth in your yard. A local rosarian suggests substituting a mixture of one-third coarse sand, one-third good soil, and one-third peat moss or compost for the original soil. (Premixed rose soil is available at garden centers.) Preferably the rose bed should be prepared in advance of planting time.

Roses should be planted about 8 to 10 inches deep and 2 feet apart. Trim out any dead or damaged roots or canes. Cut the healthy canes back to about one-quarter inch above the first healthy-looking bud. Follow the general rules for planting (see chapter 7). Be sure to eliminate any residual air pockets by tamping lightly but firmly on the soil. Mulch loosely with pine needles, leaves, or compost to help retain moisture and control weeds.

Fertilizing and Watering. Your roses should be fed about every six to eight weeks beginning in spring and ending in September, for a total of four feedings. Use a good commercial rose fertilizer or a general-purpose fertilizer such as 10-10-10. Distribute the fertilizer in a band starting about 6 inches from the crown of the plant, and extend outward to roughly 18 inches. Work in gently and water. Your soil type will dictate how frequently you will need to water. Roses do not like to dry out completely. If you have sandy soil, you may want to water as often as every three to four days in the summer months. More clayey soils should be watered about once a week. Soaker hose and drip irrigation methods are preferred, as overhead sprinkling will wet the leaves, leaving them vulnerable to fungal disease.

Diseases and Pests. The most troublesome part of raising roses is pest and disease control. Black

spot and powdery mildew are the major diseases that threaten roses in Central Texas. The leaves of plants suffering black spot display (no surprise) large black spots; then they yellow and drop. Applications of a fungicide such as Benomyl can control this condition. Frequent inspection will catch the disease in the early stages. Powdery mildew is evident by the presence of irregularly shaped spread of grayish fungal spores. Again, apply the previously recommended fungicide.

Pruning. Rosebushes are pruned to produce more and better blossoms, and for that reason their pruning needs are more demanding than those of other shrubs. Pruning begins with cutting back dead and diseased canes to the live wood, removing canes that conflict, and snipping off suckers coming up from the roots. Next, prune to shape. The rigid rose-pruning orthodoxy of years ago has been replaced by greater latitude in letting the gardener exercise judgment. Roses can be pruned high, medium, or low. While there are many opinions on what the optimal cut is, it is safe to remove one-third to one-half of the previous year's growth. The cane should be cut about a quarter-inch above an outward-pointing bud at a thirty-degree angle. When you direct the growth outward, the plant will have good sunshine and air circulation.

Hybrid teas, floribundas, and grandifloras should be pruned in the spring. Large-flowered climbers are also pruned lightly in the spring. Climbers that bloom only in the spring should be pruned after they blossom. Old roses, which can tend naturally toward a graceful shape, may need less frequent pruning than hybrid teas.

If flowers are cut, late-summer pruning often is unnecessary. Otherwise, it is advisable to prune in a similar manner, although somewhat less severely. Remember always to make your cut with a sharp tool. Ragged cuts may fail to heal properly, leaving the plants vulnerable to insects and diseases.

Despite the demanding regimen, most gardeners are tempted to try roses at one time or another because they are so beautiful. In our area you can actually have roses in bloom for nine months of the year. For many that's reason enough to grow the "queen of flowers."

 **FYI: Roses**

Earth-Kind Roses (http://earth-kindroses.tamu.edu/) provides growing tips about and photos of more than a dozen roses recommended for Texas soils and conditions. You will want to visit this site before purchasing any rosebush.

Texas Rose Rustlers (http://texasroserustlers.com/) explains the correct way to rustle, propagate, and tend roses. This caring and enthusiastic organization also provides a calendar of events.

CHAPTER 12

The Vegetable Garden

"LOCAL, FRESH, and sustainable," today's clarion call for all concerned about food production and the environment can be answered right in the backyard. Forget tainted spinach, recalled lettuce, and tasteless tomatoes. Grow your own!

All gardening in Central Texas is replete with special opportunities and challenges—vegetable gardening is no exception. Two short growing seasons and a large selection of vegetables to grow mean vegetables on the table and the gardener in the garden twelve months a year. A formidable environment of bad soil, drought, floods, and whatever else nature

doles out means a rich life full of constant learning and experimenting. This is where gardeners test their mettle.

For families the opportunities to anticipate and to learn responsibility, patience, and humility are boundless. Children learn where food comes from and how it is produced. Healthy eating is easily encouraged. And in the garden there are useful, rewarding chores for even the youngest gardener. Vegetable gardening opens the kitchen door to new cooking adventures. Vegetable gardening is simply the best gardening has to offer.

A Word about and for Community Gardens

Several years ago I lost my battle with shade in my home garden and with a friend rented a plot for growing vegetables at a community garden. I knew with full sun I would be enjoying home-grown tomatoes, peppers, and beans soon again, but I never imagined the fulfilling experience of communal gardening. Sharing seeds, tools, experience, responsibilities, and friendship has enriched my life and honed my gardening skills immeasurably. At the community garden everyone is a learner and a teacher, a contributor and a receiver. If vegetable gardening at your home is limited by lack of space, sun, or any other reason, please search for a community garden in your area. The rewards will be large and many. Your county extension agent may be able to help you locate an organization. The American Community Gardening Association is a superb resource for anyone seeking information and guidance about starting a community garden.

Vegetable Garden Essentials

Successful vegetable gardening anywhere, but especially in Central Texas, requires an understanding of and respect for the elements and how plants work.

Soil. Central Texas soils in their natural state are unsuitable for growing vegetables. Vegetable gardening requires continual amending with organic matter and regular applications of fertilizer. (See chapter 2 for a complete discussion of soil, nutrients, and soil preparation for garden use.) It is also important that your vegetable garden is on level ground to prevent runoff and ensure adequate moisture throughout the beds.

Nutrients. When we grow vegetables, we are pushing plants for maximum production—we are not letting nature take its course. In truth, fertilizing the home garden is more often guesswork than science. Unlike monoculture farming, the home garden is an assortment of several kinds of vegetables, each with its own nutrient requirements. Consider, too, the environmental factors that influence soil fertility (soil temperature and texture, moisture level, and soil pH) and the gardener's countless fertilizer choices (organic, chemical, quick release, slow release, liquid, and granular), and you begin to see that fertilizing the vegetable garden is some science, a bit art, and a lot of experience. Fortunately, for many vegetables the margin of error is generous. Getting a soil test, at least initially, and following its recommendations is the smart way to start off. Then learn as much as you can about the vegetables you choose to grow— what nutrients they need, how much, and when they need them. If you can be confident about your soil's nutrient levels, you are a step ahead.

In praise of raised beds
Building raised beds and filling them with good-quality, fertile garden soil is a great way to fast-

Permanent raised beds

track a small home vegetable garden and reduce its maintenance over the long term. Raised beds provide good soil depth and structure for root development and good drainage. Soil in raised beds warms up more quickly in spring and can be planted more intensively. Permanent raised beds are contained and defined by a frame, and the soil is in little danger of being compacted or washed away. Preparation for the next growing season involves lightly forking in fertilizer and a couple inches of compost, and you're ready to go. No tilling or reshaping beds is necessary. The extra cost of soil is offset

Temporary raised beds

by the work saved by not having to improve our native soils. Cedar boards (there are safety concerns about the use of chemically treated wood for vegetable beds), stone, and brick are good materials. Be sure the bed is level. A manageable size is 8 feet × 4 feet × 1 foot. Width and depth are more important dimensions than length. A bed wider than 4 feet will be difficult to tend.

Temporary raised beds are made by mounding and shaping the prepared and amended soil. Without the support of a frame they will erode over time and require some redoing each season. They are, however, flexible and free.

Climate. Temperatures in Central Texas can range from subfreezing in winter to searing heat waves of temperatures greater than 100°F during the summer. This is the reason we have two growing seasons, both relatively short. The spring season begins in midwinter when gardens are planned and beds are prepared. The objective of the spring garden is to grow and harvest before the searing summer heat shuts down production. In the blistering heat of the summer the soil is prepared again, this time for the fall/winter garden. Now the objective is to bring in the harvest of the more tender vegetables before the first freeze. Many of our fall garden crops are cold hardy, and their flavor is improved by cooler temperatures. Mustard, cabbage, and other greens are just a few examples. A hard frost, though, could mean the end for fall tomatoes, peppers, tender lettuces, and turnips.

The amount of sunlight in the home garden varies over the seasons; regardless of when you grow vegetables, your garden will need six to eight hours of sunlight. Although carrots, collards, spinach, lettuce, kale, and turnips may tolerate a bit of shade, vegetables just like a lot sun. Be sure to calculate the amount of sunlight the garden will receive when you make your plans.

Water. Just think how rapidly vegetables grow. A tomato, for example, is a seed in January and hopefully is producing pounds of tomatoes in June—five to six months from seed to production. Vegetable plants need a lot of water in addition to a lot of sun and fertilizer. They need to be "turgid"—full of water—throughout their productive cycle.

When to Water. After amending the soil and preparing the garden for planting, water the beds thoroughly and deeply before planting. This is critical for the encouragement of deep rooting and is especially true for the fall garden when the soil may be deeply dry after a long, hot, dry summer.

It is essential that fruiting vegetables (eggplant, tomatoes, peppers, squash, and cucumbers) receive regular watering during flowering and fruit set. Moisture shortage at this stage may result in reduced yields. Vegetables may be smaller in size if they suffer moisture shortage during the time when the fruit, roots, or heads are enlarging.

It is hard to believe there is a time when we can overwater our vegetables in Central Texas. However, it is important not to overwater when the fruit is ripening. Too much water at this stage may reduce the flavor of tomatoes, melons, and corn. When the fruit is ripening, it is no longer growing, so the size will not be affected. Water or irrigate with care at this time.

Test the soil moisture by inserting a finger into the soil. If the soil is moist at a depth of 2 inches, your moisture level is okay. You want to encourage deep rooting for good water uptake. Shallow-rooted vegetables (lettuce, radish, onions, cucumbers, peppers, spinach, squash, and cabbage) need more frequent and more shallow watering than deep-rooted crops.

Soaker hose irrigation

How to Water. Water thoroughly, but don't drown the plants. The soil should be moist, not wet. The goal is to provide a sufficient and consistent moisture level and avoid alternate periods of wet and dry. Well-maintained drip irrigation systems and soaker hoses are preferred ways to water the vegetable garden. Delivering water directly to the roots and not to the leaves, they deliver water efficiently and help reduce the chances for fungal problems. They work well with mulches, are less wasteful than overhead sprinkling, and are less time-consuming than hand watering.

Planning, Selecting, and Planting

What Shall I Grow? If you are new to vegetable gardening, it's smart to start out small and with vegetables that have a good success rate for our conditions. Of course, it doesn't make sense to grow what you don't like to eat. Vegetable gardening requires time, some investment, and work. Starting out with a successful collage of lettuces in a pot can be preferable to being overwhelmed by an ambitious instant "family farm." At community gardens, attrition rates are highest among new gardeners with grand expectations and insufficient appreciation for the work required. Try early-maturing vegetables that don't require waiting five or six months before you can put them on the table. Affirmation and quick rewards are just the encouragement beginners need.

Beets, broccoli, bush squash, cabbage, carrots, eggplant, green beans, lettuce, onions, peppers, radishes, spinach, tomatoes, and turnips are all good candidates for a small garden.

Beets, bush beans, lettuce, mustard, radishes, spinach, summer squash, and turnips mature between thirty and sixty days. Later-maturing vegetables include broccoli, carrots, cucumbers, onions, peppers, potatoes, and tomatoes. Save the cantaloupes, cauliflower, potatoes, sweet potatoes, and watermelon till you have the space and time to devote to them.

Growing Up. Training peas, cucumbers, and squashes that like to sprawl or climb to grow up on a trellis or other support system is a great way to grow these space robbers in a small garden. It also makes harvesting a lot easier. Whether you use a cage or trellis, be sure the support is well anchored in the soil.

Plants get heavy, and without good grounding they will topple in the wind.

Containers. Carrots (short varieties), eggplant, green onions, lettuce, kale, peppers, radishes, summer squash, and many tomatoes are ideally suited for containers. Not only are containers great for decks, patios, and other small spaces—they are movable. You can chase the rays or haul the containers inside at the threat of a freeze. Use a lightweight soil-less mixture for good drainage. Since many mixes have no inherent nutrient value, you will need to fertilize regularly. Pelletized slow-release or liquid fertilizers work best in container gardening. You will need to be very conscientious about watering. During the summer you may need to water twice a day.

Varieties Matter. Listen to the masters—in this case the local Master Gardeners or your county extension agent. The seed racks are brimming with tempting and popular choices perfect for Oregon, Georgia, or Connecticut. Supermarkets and hardware stores do not always have the expertise to select the appropriate varieties; at big, national chains inventory purchasing is done at the national level. Purchase varieties recommended for your area.

After you have some experience, you can venture into more exotic fare.

Getting Started. You will want to get your spring garden prepped and ready to go as early as possible. Onion sets arrive at nurseries in January, and early to mid-February is the time to plant potatoes. Years ago, gardeners did much more seed starting at home in basements and cold frames, but today we are fortunate to have a wide selection of vegetable transplants at grocery stores and farmers' markets, small nurseries and big-box stores. Even if it is still too cold to plant, buy transplants when they start arriving at market and care for them at home. This way you can avoid shopworn plants that may have received erratic watering and care. End-of-season sales are not always a bargain.

The young plants should be strong and vigorous and free of insects, disease, and injury. Inspect carefully. These plants have been growing rapidly, and it's almost impossible to avoid getting root-bound plants now and then. Experienced gardeners know these transplants are more robust than they look and will benefit from a little rough handling to loosen their roots before planting. A few broken roots will be replaced quickly once planted, but a tightly wound, compacted ball of roots will never reach out into the soil to achieve its optimum growth.

Avoid plants with soil that looks hard or dry and has withdrawn from the container walls (a clear sign they have been allowed to dry out) or have roots already emerging from the pot's bottom holes.

Seeds or Transplants? Transplants are great when you need just a few plants or want to get a jump on the season. Broccoli, cabbage, eggplant, kale, peppers, and tomatoes are examples of vegetables that work well as transplants. Direct sowing of seeds is preferable when you need a whole row of crops such as beets, carrots, lettuce, and spinach. Some plants, such as beans, cucumbers, okra, and squash, just do better grown from seed. Seed packets are packed for a given season. For best germination results select seeds that say "Sell by" or "Packed for" the season when you are planting. Store seeds in a cool place. Many gardeners keep their seeds in an airtight jar in the refrigerator.

The number of days to harvest is stated on seed packets or transplant markers. In the case of seeds, the given number of days begins when the seeds are planted in the soil. The number of days for transplants represents the number of days to harvest from the time the transplants are set out in the garden. These are estimated times. Weather, fertility, and watering practices all influence plant maturity.

When Should I Plant? Plant according to the planting guide developed for your county by the Texas A&M Agriculture Extension Service or local Master Gardeners. These planting times are based on average temperatures and are guidelines, not scripture. A good way to hedge your bets against unreliable weather is to plant your seeds early and often. Make one sowing at the earliest date of the recommended planting time span; then sow again every ten days until the end of the time span. This will also maximize your harvest time, giving you a long, steady supply of vegetables.

Beware: Soil crusting over newly planted seeds is to be avoided at all costs. It can mean the end for many of the smaller seeds, such as carrot and lettuce, but even bigger seeds like beets can be ruined. Our clay-based soils are prone to crusting, and late summer and early fall plantings are particularly vulnerable.

Mulched paths

To prevent soil crusting, cover the seeds to the recommended depth with mature compost or even potting soil instead of your garden's soil. Water gently but thoroughly. To prevent rapid evaporation and reduce soil temperature in summer and early fall, you may want to cover newly planted areas with shade cloth, or even old window screens, until the seeds have germinated. Once the plants are up, remove the protection to allow the seedlings to get sun. Continue to monitor soil moisture diligently.

Mulch. After the vegetables are up and growing for a bit, apply a 1- to 2-inch layer of mulch of clean straw, compost, or leaves to keep the soil moist and cool and discourage weeds. It is very important to water your garden thoroughly *before* adding mulch and again afterward. Some plants (tomatoes and peppers, for example) may need to be mulched several times. At the end of the season the organic mulch can be turned under, enriching the soil with much needed organic matter. The next season's soil prep has just begun.

Row Cover. More and more gardeners are resorting to row cover for cold, wind, and pest protection in their vegetable gardens. Row cover is spunbonded polyester or polypropylene

Row cover with PVC hoop supports

fabric. It comes in varying weights (0.3 to 2.0 ounces per square yard) and allows air, water, and light to pass through. Heavier-weight material gives greater cold protection (up to 7°F); lighter weights allow more light to pass through and provide good protection against birds and bugs. To be maximally effective against insects, the bottom edges of the fabric must be secured to the soil.

Use of row cover increases both soil and air temperatures, giving vegetables a good start early in the season. Protection against wind means less water loss. Row cover works best when supported by hoops made with PVC tubing or 9–10-gauge galvanized wire and with mulch and drip irrigation.

Vegetables that do very well under row cover are cole family members, cucumbers, eggplant, peppers, squash, and tomatoes. Great cold and pest protection and increased yields—so why aren't all vegetable gardens under wraps? Extra work, cost, and aesthetics belong in the equation. After installation, you have to make sure weeds or insects that have managed to breach the barrier are controlled. The warm, moist conditions are perfect not only for the vegetables but also for weeds and multiplying generations of insects. If you use row cover, be sure to provide for adequate air circulation.

The dreaded squash vine borer (larval stage of a diurnal moth that is most active in the morning) is successfully thwarted by row cover, but squash requires insect pollination to set fruit. Install row cover just as seedlings emerge and remove at bloom time to allow for pollination. Hopefully by this time the threat of the borer has passed. Under extremely hot conditions tomato and pepper yields may actually be reduced when grown under row cover.

Row cover is not very expensive, but it does add to the cost of gardening in addition to making extra work. Row cover has to be disposed of when it gets soiled and tattered (usually two to three years), which adds to the landfill.

Labels and Journals. Labels containing the variety name and date planted require little effort to make and are invaluable in tracking the garden's progress. It is difficult to overstate the importance of experience in gardening. Recording pest problems, weather, plant varieties, missteps, and smart decisions in a journal will provide useful information when planning future seasons. Revisiting past gardens

through a journal turns out to be enormously pleasurable and very often amusing.

Tending

Watering, weeding, fertilizing, and being on the lookout for insect and disease problems are the basic garden routine. Thinning vegetables is an easily overlooked but necessary chore. After putting in the effort and care to see that tender seedlings make it through, it's really hard to pluck out thriving future carrots, lettuce, and beets. No gardener enjoys this job, but it is essential for a bountiful harvest of optimally grown vegetables. Root crops need space to develop; all crops need sun and air circulation. Most thinnings are edible, which is some solace.

Fertilizing. Throughout the growing seasons vegetables will need additional applications of fertilizer. Follow the label directions for amount and frequency for side dressings or doses of liquid fertilizer. For sandy soils and container gardens, which have less moisture retention, smaller amounts at more frequent intervals are better than larger, less frequent applications. At the organic community garden, I find most vegetables do very well with two or three additional applications of a combination of equal amounts of liquid seaweed and fish emulsion.

Insects, Diseases, and Weeds. From time to time, you need to cope with invaders, insects and other critters, and diseases (see chapter 13 for a full discussion). Plastic or cardboard collars surrounding young plants to thwart cutworms, potions and elixirs concocted from foul-smelling ingredients, releasing natural predators, and companion planting with naturally repellent flowers and herbs all have devoted fans and followers. While the success of such measures is more anecdotal than scientific, it doesn't mean that it doesn't work. It is always good to listen.

If you use chemical pesticides, never exceed application levels on the label instructions. Make sure you check the label for the number of days before harvest you may apply the chemical. Since I vegetable garden at an organic community garden, any pesticides I use are Organic Materials Review Institute (OMRI) approved.

Take time each day to walk the vegetable garden. Check its progress and look for signs of trouble. While you're there, always remove a weed or two.

It is amazing how incremental weeding adds up to a weed-free garden over time. Remove from the garden any infected, infested, and old plants no longer producing. They are probably harboring diseases and insects just waiting for your next crop. Time spent in the garden is as good for your head as for your plants. And always remember, "The garden's best friend is the shadow of the gardener." It's true.

Harvesting

The crop is in. You have put in a lot of work, time, and hope. Don't lose all the benefits of freshness and superior flavor by neglecting to do the right thing at and after harvest. To be enjoyed at their best, vegetables need to be harvested at the right time and properly stored and handled.

- Vegetables harvested too early may result in a smaller yield and/or underdeveloped flavor.
- Those left too long on the vine or in the ground may become fibrous and lose flavor rapidly due to sugars converting to starches.
- Bruised and injured plants spoil more rapidly than unblemished ones.

- Harvest when foliage is dry to prevent spreading diseases.
- Do not harvest when foliage is wilted. This will only increase water stress.

Vegetable life goes on after harvest. Plants continue to respire, consuming sugars, acids, and vitamins. These changes in chemistry affect flavor, texture, and nutrient value. Slowing down life processes quickly preserves quality and prevents spoilage. The best way to slow respiration and reduce water loss is to keep vegetables cool. Harvest early in the day, when it is cooler and vegetables have higher water content. Always keep harvested vegetables out of direct sun.

Rinse vegetables under the hose immediately after harvest.

This will start the cooling process and prevent a lot of dirt coming into the house, too. In the house, wash thoroughly. A splash or two of vinegar in the rinsing water brings many errant bugs to the water's surface, but don't count on it to catch everything. If you do not rinse thoroughly, you could end up serving an unintentional side of aphids at dinner. Inspect and inspect again.

Drain and/or spin dry in a salad spinner. This is great for all the greens, but you can spin just about anything that will fit in the spinner. Then pack in zippered, plastic bags with a piece of paper towel and as much air pressed out as possible. Store in the hydrator drawer of the refrigerator. Lettuce will remain fresh for a week or longer. Root crops will last for weeks.

VEGETABLE FAMILIES

Nightshade Family					
eggplant	pepper	potato	tomato		
Brassica or Cole Family					
Broccoli	Brussels sprouts	Cabbage	Cauliflower	Collards	Kale
Kohlrabi	Radish	Turnip			
Goosefoot Family					
Beets	Spinach	Swiss chard			
Gourd Family					
Cantaloupe	Cucumber	Pumpkin	Summer squash	Watermelon	Winter squash
Lily Family					
Garlic	Leek	Onion	Shallot		

Postharvest

After harvesting, remove residual plant material from the garden and maintain good sanitation practices. If you have suffered from insect invasions and diseases, discard the debris in the trash. Admittedly, there is no greater at-one-with-the-universe feeling for a gardener than starting the next season by putting the remainder of the previous one in the compost. But, in truth, we tend to be pretty casual about home compost management, and the piles do not reliably reach killing temperatures throughout. You could end up incubating the next epidemic or generation of pests.

Mulch to prevent weeds and moderate soil temperature.

Plant cover crops if the garden is going to be fallow for some time. Cover crops improve soil quality, enhance nitrogen management, and hold the soil. They

Summer harvest

also discourage weeds, insects, and nematodes. Good summer cover crops are black-eyed peas and buckwheat. In fall, plant cereal (Elbon) rye if you have had nematode problems, annual rye, or clover. Be sure to till or fork in the cover crop (green manure) before it goes to seed. Elbon rye, a tough customer indeed, should be tilled in before it reaches a foot high or you probably won't be able to do it. Allow the cover crop to decompose about three weeks before preparing the garden for the next season. Keep the area moist to speed decomposition.

Crop Rotation

Presumably, the home vegetable garden is planted with a variety of vegetables from a number of different plant families. To maintain the advantage of this diverse environment over the uniformity of large farm monoculture, it is important to practice crop rotation. Without it, crops grown repeatedly in the same location will eventually lose vitality and decline in productivity. Increasingly, they will be subject to these problems:

- Nematodes and soil insects
- Essential mineral imbalance
- Reduced organic matter
- Soil-borne diseases

Briefly, vegetables of the same family, for example, eggplant, pepper, potato, and tomato, are vulnerable to the same diseases and insects. You will improve your chances for a successful, productive crop if you avoid planting members of the same family for two or three successive years in the same rows or beds.

My Favorite Spring Garden

The spring garden consists mainly of fruit-bearing vegetables.

Beans. There are lots of bean varieties for Central Texas—bush, lima, and pole. Beans are cold sensitive and like to be planted in warm, loose soil. Wait until about four weeks or so after the last frost to plant. Most beans may be planted again later in summer. Beans need regular watering throughout the season, but it is especially critical when plants are in bloom. If you can, avoid getting the leaves wet when watering. Rust and powdery mildew are potential problems, so drip irrigation is an excellent choice for the bean patch.

Planting and Tending: Plant bush bean seeds 1 to 1½ inches deep about 1 inch apart. When they emerge, thin to 3 inches.

Rows should be 2 to 3 feet apart. Pole beans are best grown up tepees of three or four poles. Two to three seeds should be planted at the base of each pole. They can also be grown up trellises or walls.

Harvesting: Beans that are picked when too mature will be starchy and of poor quality. Pick snap beans when the pods are full and seeds are visible but not bulging. Pole beans are at their best when pods are full and seeds are about one-fourth grown. If you pick frequently, bean plants will produce tender, more flavorful beans over a long time.

Cucumbers. Cucumbers are good candidates for vertical or container gardening. They tend to sprawl and take up a lot of space unless trained to grow up. They need loose soil rich in organic matter and plenty of water. Other than that, they are not particularly difficult plants to grow. Misshapen or collapsed fruit is an indication of inadequate pollination. The heat-tolerant Asian variety 'Suhyo Cross' hybrid is a superb performer in Central Texas. It has few seeds and unsurpassed flavor.

Planting and Tending: Plant about six seeds in a "hill" (mounded-up soil). When plants emerge, thin to three. A side dressing once during the growing season is helpful but not necessary. Cucumbers are heavy drinkers, so be sure they receive adequate water.

Harvesting: Cucumbers are ready to pick when the skin is bright green and the seeds are still soft. Pick older, dull, and yellowing cucumbers to encourage new fruit development. Refrigerate cucumbers immediately. Place in a paper bag and store in the crisper compartment to slow moisture loss.

Eggplant. I grew my first eggplant not because I liked eggplant but because I loved and admired its beauty—the pleasing shapes; smooth, satiny skin; and rich colors. Then I learned there was so much more to appreciate. Mild taste and soft flesh make it a perfect complement for other vegetables, sauces, spices, and herbs. It is excellent grilled, fried, or baked. Extremely heat tolerant and productive, Asian varieties 'Ichiban' and 'Pingtung Long' are excellent choices for Central Texas gardens.

Planting and Tending: Eggplant is a warm-season plant that does well from transplants. It likes soil enriched with organic matter. Use a starter solution

'Ichiban' Eggplant

(half fish emulsion, half liquid seaweed) at the time of planting. Susceptible to cold damage, eggplant should be transplanted when the temperature is 65°F. Eggplant should be watered consistently during the growing season and mulched. Critical time for irrigation is from bloom through fruit set.

Harvesting: Pick eggplant when the fruit is glossy (don't let it grow dull on the plant) and springy to the touch. Store eggplant in a paper bag in the crisper section of the refrigerator.

Okra

ARGENTINIAN GRILLED
EGGPLANT

3 long Asian eggplants
2 cloves garlic, minced
3 tbs olive oil
1 tsp dried oregano or
several sprigs fresh
1 tsp dried basil or several
sprigs fresh
½ tsp dried oregano or
several sprigs fresh
Salt and pepper to taste

1. Heat grill to hot.
2. Leave on the stems and cut
   eggplants in half length-
   wise. Mix garlic and oil in
   a small bowl. Brush mix-

ture over cut sides of the
eggplants. Mix herbs and
spices together in a bowl
and set aside.

3. Arrange eggplants, cut side
   down, on a hot grill until
   nicely browned, 3–4 minutes.
4. Lightly brush the skin sides
   of the eggplants with the oil
   mixture. Using tongs, turn
   eggplants and brush with
   remaining oil and garlic.
   Sprinkle with herbs and
   salt and pepper.
5. Continue cooking, cut sides
   up, 6–8 minutes until flesh
   is soft.
6. Serve immediately. Hold
   the stem in one hand and
   scrape flesh from skin in a
   sweeping motion.

Adapted from Steven
Raichlen's *The Barbecue
Bible*

Okra. If you grow vegetables
in Texas and don't already like
okra, it's to your advantage to
acquire a taste for it. When a
dreadful summer seems to wipe
out everything else, the okra
is still there, standing tall and
producing its lovely hibiscus
blossoms and pods almost faster
than you can harvest. Like oth-

ers, I was skittish about okra until a friend insisted I try just one bright green 2-inch pod parboiled for thirty seconds and sprinkled with coarse sea salt. It was amazingly light with a clean, crisp flavor and has become a favorite. Okra goes well with tomatoes, onions, and peppers. It can be pickled; used in stews, soups, and salads; or stand on its own. A member of the mallow family (hibiscus and cotton are relatives), okra is one of our most heat- and drought-tolerant vegetables. While best yields are produced in well-drained, fertile soil, okra is more forgiving of poor soil and patchy watering practices than most other vegetables.

Planting and Tending: Soak okra seeds overnight, and plant 1 inch deep and 2 inches apart. Thin until the plants are 1 foot apart. Be on the lookout for stink bugs and aphids. Fertilize after the first harvest.

Harvesting: Many garden guides recommend picking okra when the pods are between 3 and 4 inches. Personally, I prefer 2 to 3 inches. Okra grows rapidly and quickly turns woody and fibrous. Okra will keep three to five days in the refrigerator, but it is spectacular when eaten the same day as harvest.

Peppers. Whether a sweet banana or a hot jalapeño, peppers like our heat and sun. Make sure that they are planted where they receive a full six to eight hours of it. Peppers, like all vegetables, like water, especially when in bloom and during the fruit swell, but they do not like to sit in it. Make sure they have good drainage.

Since peppers set fruit in temperatures up to about 90°F, it is best to use transplants rather than seeds. Planting seeds late enough to avoid freeze will bring plants into bloom after temperatures have climbed above the 90° mark, and they may not produce any fruit. At the other end of the thermometer, peppers will be damaged if the soil temperature drops below the mid-50s. Peppers do best in soil amended with lots of organic matter. Garden fertilizer (1-2-1 ratio) added before planting will also get pepper plants off to a good start. Peppers are subject to mosaic virus, whose symptoms include stunted growth, yellowing, and hard shriveled leaves. The best control is to remove affected plants. Spider mites also can attack peppers. Sun scald can be identified by whitish spots on the surface of the fruit. Not much can be done about it, but the quality and taste are not affected.

Planting and Tending: Set out transplants about 18 to 24 inches apart in rows 24 inches apart. Plant after all danger of frost has passed and as soon as the soil is warm. Side-dress with a high-nitrogen fertilizer every month. Keep plants well watered, but not soggy. The larger pepper plants do well with the support of a cage. Conical cages sold as tomato cages, which are really much too small for most tomatoes, are perfect for peppers. After peppers bloom, begin applying mulch regularly throughout the growing season.

Harvesting: Pick when color is bright and fruit is firm, not shriveled.

Potatoes. There is something so appealing about growing potatoes. Maybe the reason is that they are so earthy and basic, or maybe that we don't get to see them until we dig in to harvest. There are only two varieties (white Kennebec and red La Soda) that are reliable here. Potatoes take up lots of space, so plan your garden carefully. I once thought a potato was a potato but later discovered that homegrown potatoes are truly better.

Seed potatoes start showing up at nurseries in January. They can get picked over in the store rather quickly, so it's a good idea to buy them early and keep them cool and dry at home. The garage will do nicely. Mid-February is the time to get them in the ground. Small seed potatoes can be planted singly; larger potatoes should be cut into three pieces with two to three eyes in each piece. Dust them with dusting sulfur a couple of days before planting as a precaution against fungal disease.

Planting: Soil preparation is key. Work lots of composted manure or compost deeply into the soil. Dig a trench 6 to 8 inches deep, and set the seed potatoes 12 inches apart. Cover with 4 inches of soil.

Tending: When the potato plants are 8 inches tall, cover them with soil until only the top 4 inches of the plants are exposed. This is called "dirting" or "hilling" the potatoes. This is where the new tubers will grow. If potatoes are exposed to sunlight for a prolonged time, they will turn green and become bitter, so be sure to keep them covered at all times. Keep the soil moist but not wet until the plants bloom. After they blossom, they can get along with a bit less water. At this point you want to slow their growth to prevent splits, bumps, and "hollow heart."

Harvesting: You can take "new" potatoes when they reach 1 to 2 inches, while the plants are still growing. Harvest mature potatoes after the vines have died. Avoid harvesting in wet soil. If the soil is wet, wait until it dries before digging. The potatoes will be fine. One grower recommends leaving the potatoes in the ground for two weeks after the vines have died back before harvesting to allow them to cure a bit. This will protect them against bruising and can prolong storage life. At the community garden we have inadvertently unearthed potatoes that had evaded harvest months earlier, and they were perfectly delicious. Finding the potatoes and not damaging them when digging them out can be a challenge. A hay fork, with its long, skinny tines, works better than a spading fork. Approach the plants from the side, insert the fork gently, and turn over the soil to expose the potatoes. Store in a cool, dark place with good air circulation. Do not refrigerate. In cold temperatures potato starch will convert to sugar, giving the potatoes an off, sweet taste. Potatoes hold up well stored for weeks at room temperature.

Summer Squash

Summer Squash. Whether yellow crookneck, straightneck, or zucchini, summer squash is easy to grow (if you are fortunate enough to escape the dreaded squash vine borer) and so versatile in the kitchen.

Planting: Squash can be planted either in "hills" or in rows. Follow the seed packet directions for spacing. Squash seeds are large, easy to handle, and germinate quickly. Squash started from seed seem to do better than transplants. The plants are rapid growers and are often too large for their containers before being purchased. Squash like fertile, well-drained soil. They are very cold sensitive and should be planted three to four weeks after the last frost.

Celebrity Tomatoes

Tending: Squash are shallow rooted and need frequent, light waterings. They should receive even moisture throughout the season.

Harvesting: For the best squash, pick while still young and tender and glossy, up to 6 to 8 inches in length and 1½ to 2 inches in diameter. Summer squash is usually ready to pick four to eight days after flowering.

BASIL-INFUSED SQUASH

1. Wash and slice yellow squash in ½-inch slices.
2. Bring a skillet with ¼ inch of water to a simmering boil.
3. Add the squash slices and cook 15–30 seconds.
4. Add a handful of basil, cover, remove from heat, and let steep 30 seconds.
5. Drain, add salt and pepper to taste, and serve immediately.

Suggested by Susan Hoberman, Austin

Tomatoes. Tomatoes are the most popular home garden vegetable. They truly excite gardeners. More discussion, work, and dreams go into growing tomatoes than any other vegetable. There are hundreds of varieties in a multitude of shapes and sizes and a rainbow of colors from black (sort of) to white (yes). They are relatively easy to grow but prickly enough to present a formidable challenge. Good tomatoes are undeniably delicious and are their own reward, but I doubt gardeners would be so obsessed about growing them if it weren't for that challenge. The 'Sweet Million' and 'Sun Gold' tomatoes that produce prodigiously and endlessly with little effort never command the attention and respect we lavish on an iffy heirloom or fussy exotic.

The amount of information, instructions, and opinion about growing tomatoes can be dizzying and intimidating for a beginner. Relax and realize that there are many valid ways to grow tomatoes. Go to good (local) resources for your information and do your best. Next year you can try something else.

Tomatoes require lots of sun, good drainage, fertile soil, and a uniform supply of water. Excessive moisture fluctuations can result in blossom end rot, a dark discoloration at the tip of the tomato, and cracking. Failure to set fruit, a common and dispiriting occurrence, can be the result of daytime temperatures above 90°F and nighttime temperatures above 70°F. Other factors may be excessive or insufficient nutrition, insects (especially aphids and thrips), and disease.

Certainly tomatoes can be grown in fall, but it's a gamble against the weather, and I think they are a low-percentage fall crop. You have to plant and nurse along new transplants in the midst of summer's inferno and then be ever hopeful that that early norther never comes. There is only so much heartache you can tolerate in a growing season.

Tomatoes are classified as determinate, indeterminate, and semi-determinate. Determinate tomatoes grow to a certain size (3 to 3½ feet), produce fruit, and decline. Many popular early-maturing varieties such as 'BHN 444' and 'Early Girl' are determinate. Indeterminates (6 to 10 feet) can go on growing until they are killed by frost. While they may produce longer than determinates, the Texas heat will shut them down eventually. 'Better Boy,' 'Porter's Pride,' and 'Sun Gold' are indeterminates. Falling somewhere in between is the ever-popular semi-determinate (3 to 5 feet) 'Celebrity.'

Winter Greens

Select varieties recommended for your area. Our short seasons require tomato plants that reach maturity early and produce quickly. Choose plants listed as "VFNTM" resistant. This means that they are not susceptible to verticillium wilt, fusarium wilt, nematodes, and tobacco mosaic, all of which are deadly to the plants. Pick healthy-looking plants with sturdy stems, about the thickness of a pencil.

Planting: When to set out tomato plants in the garden is always an agonizing decision. Mid-March is as good a suggestion as any. Then expect anything to happen.

- Add a couple tablespoons of tomato fertilizer or cotton-seed meal to the prepared hole.
- Remove lower leaves, leaving a tomato plant with at least three branches coming out near the top of the stem, and set in plants as deeply as possible. All those fuzzy hairs on the stem of a tomato are potential roots that will develop into a deep, strong root system to carry it into the summer. Plants should be set 3 feet apart.
- Backfill with compost-enriched soil, and shape the soil into a basin so water collects around the plant.
- Place a tomato cage (at least 24 inches in diameter) over the plant, and secure the cage to the ground with stakes to prevent it from being blown over.
- Wrap the cage in row cover, and secure it to the cage with clothespins or clamps. The covered cage will do three things: (1) it will allow temperatures inside the cage to heat up during the day but dissipate during the night, jumpstarting plant growth; (2) it will protect the plant from airborne mites that carry the leaf curl virus (a deadly one); and (3) it will protect young plants from drying, early spring winds. When daytime temperatures begin to stay in the 80s, remove the row cover. The tomato plants will be substantially larger and further along than those planted later, or without the benefit of the row cover.

Tending: Even watering, mulching, and fertilizing two to three times during the growing season are the main chores. Add a couple inches of mulch when you fertilize, and add a little more mulch each time you fertilize thereafter. Monitoring for insects and disease and out-smarting mockingbirds and other varmints complete the to-do list.

Harvesting: Tomatoes continue to ripen after they are picked, although once the tomato is picked, the sugars will not de-velop quite as well as they would have on the vine. In Central Texas we can count on steady 90° days in June. Above 86°F toma-toes' ability to turn red is greatly reduced, and the tomatoes may have an orange cast. If you har-vest the tomato when it is in the pink stage and allow it to ripen, it will be just fine. Picking at the pink stage is also the best way to outsmart the mockingbirds, who love tomatoes passionately and have an uncanny ability to judge the perfect moment for harvest. If you wait, you can't beat them.

Do *not* store fresh, unsliced tomatoes in the refrigerator—they will lose flavor within an hour. If a freeze is forecast for your fall tomatoes, pick those toma-toes without cracks, nicks, and bruises and that are light green, turning white. Hang them upside down in a cool, dark place to ripen. They will keep for a couple of months under the right conditions.

OVEN-ROASTED 'JULIETS'

The 'Juliet,' a 1999 All-American Selections Winner, is an elongated cherry tomato that produces firm, perfect tomatoes early on and until long after others have given up. The long, slow cooking brings out its rich tomato flavor, making it ideal for hors d'oeuvres or pizzalike snacks. It is also excellent with eggs.

2 lb 'Juliet' tomatoes, cut in
    half lengthwise
3 sprigs fresh thyme or 1 tsp
    dried
Pinch of confectioner's
    sugar
Pinch of salt and white
    pepper

1. Heat oven to 200°.
2. Arrange tomato halves on an aluminum foil–covered baking sheet, skin side down. Sprinkle lightly with remaining ingredients.
3. Cook for 2 hours. Turn them over and cook for 1 more hour.
4. Cool thoroughly before serving.

Kay Kitzmiller, Austin

FYI: Tomatoes

Travis County Extension Agent Skip Richter's "Growing Tomatoes Organically" originally appeared in *Texas Gardener.* Inspiring and easy to follow, it is a superb primer on growing tomatoes (http://www.texasgardener.com/pastissues/janfeb02/tomatorganic.html).

Together these two Texas A&M Aggie Horticulture Web sites answer just about every question you have or will have about raising tomatoes. The easy Q&A format is direct and clear and allows you to find the information you are seeking quickly.

Tomato Q&A, Questions 1–41 (http://aggie-horticulture.tamu.edu/plantanswers/vegetables/tomato.html)

Tomato Q&A, Questions 42–54 (http://aggie-horticulture.tamu.edu/plantanswers/vegetables/tomat2.html).

My Favorite Fall Garden

The fall garden provides root vegetables for hearty dishes and winter salads.

Beets. Beets are not only an easy crop but they are entirely edible. Young leaves are great fresh in salads or cooked. Roots are delicious boiled, roasted, or pickled. Since they are easy to grow, many gardeners plant too many beets and end up with a harvest they can neither eat nor give away. Rather than planting one large crop, try sowing small areas several weeks apart.

Planting and Tending: Plant seeds ½ inch deep in rows about 1 inch apart in loose, compost-enriched soil, and side-dress with fertilizer at least once during the growing season. Thin to 3 inches if harvesting the root, and 2 inches if harvesting the leaves. The beet "seed" you plant from the packet is really a dried fruit that contains up to six real seeds. This is the reason seedlings emerge so close to one another no matter how rigorously you follow the planting directions. To avoid disturbing the tender new roots, it is better to snip off the seedling you intend to thin instead of pulling it out of the soil. Plant flea beetles, grubworms, and wireworms can be problems.

Harvesting: For greens, pick when young and tender. Harvest roots when they are 2 to 3 inches wide at the shoulder.

JUST FOR YOU BEET SALAD

4–5 beets, preferably organically home- or community-
garden grown
⅓ cup red wine and olive
oil vinaigrette
1 small onion, preferably
1015 organically home-
grown
1 orange
Dijon mustard

1. Prepare beets your favorite
   way, and peel while still
   warm.
2. Prepare ⅓ cup of red wine
   and olive oil vinaigrette.
3. Mix one-half of vinaigrette
   with warm beets and set
   aside.
4. Shave a desired amount
   of onion, and section the
   orange.
5. Combine with beets.
6. Add a dab of Dijon mustard
   to remaining vinaigrette,
   and add to the beet, onion,
   and orange combination.

Broccoli. Prepare the soil with organic matter, and add some fertilizer to get the young plants off to a good start. Fall planting should begin in late summer. Remember that the plants are cold hardy and do well in cool conditions. If we have a mild winter, you may be able to harvest until spring. If you have never seen a broccoli plant in flower, it might be fun to let one go to seed.

Planting and Tending: Space transplants 18 to 24 inches apart in rows 36 inches apart. Mulch well. Side-dress with fertilizer twice during the growing season. Watch for aphids and harlequin bugs.

Harvesting: Cut broccoli when the head is fully developed, bright green, and still tightly closed. But it's not over just because the main head is gone. Continue harvesting side shoots as they develop. They are delicious, and harvesting them helps extend production.

Cabbage. Cabbage tolerates temperature fluctuations and clay soil! Every Central Texas garden should have at least one. Warm temperatures may cause the heads to split. Good in stews, soups, and slaws, it is one of our most versatile vegetables.

Planting and Tending: Space transplants 18 to 24 inches apart. A heavy nitrogen user, cabbage should be given additional applications of fish emulsion and/or liquid seaweed during the season. Be on guard for aphid and looper attacks. Keep soil moist.

Harvesting: Pick when heads are firm and leaves are tight. Do not wait for a monster cabbage—the head may split or crack.

Carrots. All vegetables love good, fertile, friable soil; for carrots it is essential. Tiny and persnickety, carrot seed is doomed if the soil is allowed to crust. Take extra time to work the soil to a depth of 10 to 12 inches. Remove all rocks and hard clumps of clay, which can distort the carrots. The good thing about carrots is once you get them up and going, they are seldom bothered by insects or disease. And they can be sown from September through mid-November and again late January through February, providing a nice long succession of carrots. Buy shorter varieties for best results in Central Texas soils.

Planting and Tending: Be sure the soil is moist before planting the seed. A thin layer of compost makes a nice planting surface. Space seeds according to seed packet instructions, and gently but firmly press the seed into the compost. Cover seeds with compost or sand, and keep moist until germination (14 to 21 days, longer than many other vegetables). Cover with shade cloth or a window screen until the seeds germinate to help pre-

vent crusting. When the plants are about four to eight weeks old, thin to about 2 inches apart. Side-dress with fertilizer after thinning.

Harvesting: Pull carrots when they are ½ to ¾ inch at the shoulder.

Collards. Super easy and super nutritious, a few collard plants can go a long way. With roots 2 feet long, they appreciate deep, well-drained soil. They are heavy nitrogen users.

Planting and Tending: How you harvest might determine whether you use seeds or transplants. If you harvest the entire plant all at once, you may want to plant seeds. If you harvest several leaves at a time, you might need only three to five transplants. Set out transplants in late summer to early fall. Give collards additional applications of fish emulsion and/or liquid seaweed to keep leaves nice and green. Water well. Watch out for aphids, harlequin bugs, and cabbage worms.

Harvesting: You can take entire plants when they are 6 to 10 inches tall or just the bottom leaves of plants 10 to 12 inches in height and allow the plant to continue to grow. A light frost makes collards taste sweeter.

Kale. Like other brassicas, kale is quite easy to grow. Two favorites are 'Lacinato' (sometimes called dinosaur or Tuscan kale) with crinkled blue-green leaves and the chewy Russian red kale. Both are excellent in soups and stews.

Planting and Tending: Set out transplants in late summer to mid-fall. Give kale additional applications of fish emulsion and/or liquid seaweed to keep leaves nice and green. Water well. Watch out for aphids and harlequin bugs.

Harvesting: Kale is at its most tender when the midrib is small and the leaves are not too large.

PORTUGUESE GREEN SOUP

1½ tbs olive oil
1 medium onion, minced
2 cloves garlic, minced
4–5 medium potatoes, peeled and thinly sliced
2 quarts cold water or 1½ quarts water and ½ cup chicken stock
6 oz linguica or chorizo sausage, thinly sliced
1½ tsp salt
ground black pepper to taste
4 cups kale, rinsed and julienned
2 tbs fresh lemon juice

1. In a large saucepan over

Red Russian Kale

medium-low heat, cook onion and garlic in 1½ tbs olive oil for 5–10 minutes. Stir in potatoes and cook, stirring constantly, 3 minutes more. Pour in water, bring to a boil, and let boil gently for 15–20 minutes, until potatoes are mushy.

2. Meanwhile, in a large skillet over medium-low heat, cook sausage until it has released most of its fat, about 10 minutes. Drain.

3. Mash the potato mixture with a hand blender or in a food processor. Leave some potato chunks for texture. Stir in the sausage, salt, and pepper into the soup, and return to medium heat. Cover and simmer 5 minutes.

4. Just before serving, stir kale into soup and simmer, 5 minutes, until kale is tender and jade green. Stir in the lemon juice and serve immediately.

Adapted from Irma S. Rombauer, Marion Rombauer Becker, and Ethan Becker's *Joy of Cooking: All about Soups and Stews*

Leaf Lettuce. This salad favorite is so easy and quick to grow that one can sow seed in flower beds or pots. Pill bugs love the new leaves, so be on guard. Recommended varieties are essential to avoid untimely bolting (the plant begins to form a seed head and the lettuce turns bitter). For an attractive color and leaf texture mix, plant several varieties together, such as 'Black-seeded Simpson,' 'Oak Leaf,' and 'Red Sails.'

Planting and Tending: Rake the area to be planted, and broadcast the seed. Cover the seed with a light sprinkling of soil or sifted compost, and water in. When plants emerge, they may be thinned by gently drawing a garden rake through the lettuce patch in intersecting directions. This will thin the plot and provide some early, tender lettuce. Fertilize lightly and water.

Harvesting: Harvest when leaves are small and tender up until they grow bitter. You can harvest the whole plant or just take the leaves you need from several plants. Wash and store in the refrigerator immediately.

Mustard. There is nothing like the peppery flavor of mustard to spice up the blandest of dishes. Mustard leaves can be flat or crinkly. They are superb in

Leaf Lettuces

stir-fry dishes, with onions and garlic. They grow beautifully in Central Texas. Their flavor tends to get stronger in the warmer weather. As the plants grow old, they may attract harlequin bugs and cabbage worms. It's a good idea to remove old plants when they begin to look ratty and the flavor is no longer prime.

Planting and Tending: Plant seeds ½ inch deep. Thin seedlings to 3 to 5 inches apart. Thinnings are delicious. Keep watered and fertilized.

Harvesting: Everything about mustard is easy, including harvest—just keep picking.

Onions. Onions are classified as either "short-day" or "long-day." Short-day onions are rec-

ommended for southern states and begin to bulb when there are ten to twelve hours of sunlight. You can plant seeds in late September to mid-October or put

'Southern Giant Curled' Mustard

out sets beginning in late January. Sets should be pencil width or smaller. Onions from either seeds or sets will mature in mid-May to June. Try to get the sweet onion 'Texas Grano 1015Y' sets or seeds—it's our state vegetable and is so good.

Planting and Tending: Raised beds with compost-enriched soil are ideal for growing onions. Fertilize prior to planting with a balanced (10-10-10) fertilizer. Seeds should be planted ¼ inch deep; sets, about 1 inch deep and 4 inches apart. Adequate fertilizer during the season is very important. Onions should receive their first high-nitrogen fertilizer application three weeks after planting and then every two to three weeks until the neck begins to feel soft. At this point stop fertilizing. Keep soil evenly moist, and remember to water well after each fertilizer application. Bulbs will need space to expand, so be mindful of thinning chores. Delicious thinnings can be used as scallions or green onions.

Harvesting: Harvest when the tops are yellow and about three-fourths of the leaves have fallen over. Bulb rot is a risk if you let all the tops fall. Green onions can be taken as needed. Store newly harvested onions where they can get good air circulation. Sweeter onion varieties have a shorter shelf life than the strong-tasting varieties.

Pak Choy, Bok Choi. Members of the brassica family, mild-tasting Chinese cabbages are excellent cool-weather plants with good bolt resistance. The upright heads are formed of loose, dark green leaves with thick, crisp, white or light green ribs.

Planting and Tending: Set out transplants in late summer to early fall. These crops like even moisture and do well with two or three additional applications of fish emulsion and/or liquid seaweed.

Harvesting: Harvest complete heads or by the leaf as needed.

Radish. Easy, quick, and full of flavor, radishes are a favorite in every garden. They take up little space and can be tucked into small spaces around other crops provided they are not shaded by taller plants. Sow seeds in late winter or late summer, and make successive sowings in two- to three-week intervals for a long harvest. Radishes are ready to harvest in about thirty days.

Planting and Tending: Sow seeds about ½ inch deep in rows 1 foot apart; thin to 2 inches apart as soon as the seeds germinate (since they grow so quickly, early thinning is necessary for selected plants to develop properly). Radishes have few insect or disease problems as long as good cultural practices are followed.

Harvesting: Harvest when root shoulders are 1 to 1½ inches.

Spinach. Spinach is definitely a cool-season crop. It grows well as a spring crop when it can be planted in late winter, but it tends to bolt in early summer. As a fall crop, it does quite well, its hardiness taking it into winter. It is quite possible to have a lettuce and spinach salad from your garden for Thanksgiving. But how to beat the summer heat, since spinach will not germinate in hot weather? The trick is to soak the seeds for twenty-four to forty-eight hours in water stored in the refrigerator.

Planting and Tending: Plant spinach ½ inch deep and about 2 inches apart in rows 18 inches apart. After the plants start growing, thin to 8 or 9 inches apart. Seeds can also be broadcast and then covered with soil. Whether you choose rows or the broadcast method, tamp the soil down after sowing to ensure soil contact. Spinach, particularly fall grown, is attractive to aphids—very attractive. Remove

affected leaves or treat with an insecticide. But make sure that you monitor the crop regularly—aphids just keep coming. White rust and blue mold are common foliage diseases. Remove affected leaves.

Harvesting: Start taking leaves when they are dark green and small to medium-sized.

Swiss Chard. Swiss chard is easy to grow in Central Texas and is a good substitute for the fussier spinach. A few plants will provide generously for a family for a long, long season. Erect with large dark green leaves on thick white, red, or yellow stems, chard is handsome enough to be grown in a border, flower bed, or container. Swiss chard is relatively pest-free.

Planting and Tending: Plant in well-drained, compost-enriched soil. For the spring, garden seed can be planted two to six weeks before the last average freeze date. In fall, plant seeds twelve to sixteen weeks before the first average frost date. Transplants can be set out in late winter, early spring, and again in late summer and fall. Give additional applications of fish emulsion and/or liquid seaweed throughout the season.

Harvesting: Harvest when leaves are young and tender.

Swiss Chard

Turnips. Turnips joined the regulars on my vegetable plate the day I discovered 'Hakurei,' a hybrid from Kitazawa Seed Company, a mostly Asian vegetable seed source in Oakland, California. These turnips are snow white, tender, and mild. Sautéed in butter or raw in salads, they are simply wonderful. They mature in thirty-five days.

Planting and Tending: Plant turnip seeds ½ inch deep in mid-September through mid-October. Thin to 5 inches apart. Keep plants evenly moist throughout the season. Apply fish emulsion and/or liquid seaweed once or twice during the season.

Harvesting: For turnip greens, harvest when the plants are young, well before the root is mature. For roots, harvest when the root shoulders are 2 to 3 inches across. Cool weather will improve flavor.

Vegetable Varieties for Central Texas

Asparagus: Jersey Gem, Jersey Giant, UC 157

Beans, bush: Blue Lake, Contender, Greencrop, Tendercrop, Topcrop

Beans, lima bush: Florida Butter, Henderson Bush, Jackson Wonder

Beans, pinto: Luna, Pinto 111

Beans, pole: Jade, Kentucky Wonder, Stringless Blue Lake

Beets: Asgrow Wonder, Detroit Dark Red, Pacemaker, Ruby Queen

Broccoli: Emerald Pride, Emperor, Green Comet, Green Magic, Lucky, Packman, Premium Crop

Brussels sprouts: Catskill, Jade Cross, Valiant

Cabbage: Blue Vantage, Bravo, Early Jersey Wakefield, Early Round Dutch, Globe, Red Rock; red: Rio Verde, Savoy King

Cabbage, Chinese: Jade Pagoda, Michili

Cantaloupe: Ambrosia, Caravelle, Cruiser, Israeli, Mission, Perlita, TAM Dew, TAM Uvalde

Carrot: Danvers 126, Imperator, Nantes, Orlando Gold, Purple/Maroon Dragon, Red Core, Texas Gold Spike

Cauliflower: Snowball Improved, Snow Crown, Snow King

Corn: Bonanza, Calumet, Golden Security, Kandu Korn, Merit, Summer Sweet, Sweet G-90; white: Country Gentleman, Silver Queen

Cucumber, pickling: Calypso, Carolina, Liberty, Multipik, National Pickling, Piccadilly, Salty, Sweet Success

Cucumber, slicers: Ashley, Burpless, County Fair, Dasher II, Palomar, Patio Pick, Poin-sett, Poinsett 76, Spacemaster, Straight 8, Sweet Slice, Sweet Success, Victory Hybrid

Eggplant: Black Beauty, Ichiban, Nadia, Prospero

Lettuce, butterhead: Buttercrunch, Summer Bibb, Tendercrisp

Lettuce, leaf: Black-seeded Simpson, Oakleaf, Prizehead, Red Sails, Ruby, Salad Bowl

Lettuce, romaine: Paris Island, Valmaine

Okra: Cajun Delight, Clemson 80, Clemson Spineless, Star of David

Onion: Evergreen Bunching, Granex (yellow and white), Granex 33, Texas Grano 1015Y, Texas Grano 502

Pea, edible pod: Sugar Ann, Sugar Bon, Sugar Snap

Pea, southern: Burgundy (purple hull), California No. 5, Champion (cream), Cream 40, Texas Pinkeye, Zipper Cream

Pepper, hot: Hot Jalapa, Hot Jalapeño, Hungarian Wax, Long Red or Thin Cayenne, TAMU Mild Jalapeño, Texas Serrano

Pepper, sweet: Big Bertha, Emerald Giant, Jupiter, Keystone Giant, Sweet Banana, Yolo Wonder

Potato, Irish: Kennebec (white), Red Lasoda (red)

Potato, sweet: Beauregard Centennial, Jewel

Radish: Black Spanish, Champion, Cherry Belle, Early Scarlet Globe (short top), Red Prince, Sparkler, White Chinese, White Icicle (winter)

Spinach: Bloomsdale, Dixie Savoy, Early Hybrid 7, Melody

Squash, summer: Cougar, Dixie Hybrid Crookneck, Early Prolific Straightneck, Multipik, Patty Pan, Sunburst

Squash, winter: Acorn, Butternut

Swiss Chard: Bright Lights, Lucullus, Rhubarb Chard

Tomato, cherry type: Red Cherry, Small Fry, Sun Gold, Sweet 100

Tomato, standard: Better Boy, BHN 444, Bonus, Carnival, Celebrity, Early Girl, Florida 47 & 91, Spring Giant, Sunchief, SunLeaper, Surefire, Top Gun

Herbs

Most herbs are easy to grow when their undemanding requirements of well-drained soil and lots of sun are met. They need little fertilizer and are largely disease- and pest-free. Thyme and rosemary can be used in the landscape as ground covers and in borders. They make perfect container plants. The list of herbs that can be grown in Central Texas is very long indeed. Following is a list of kitchen basics. If possible, it's nice to have them close to the kitchen door.

Basil. Basil comes in a great variety of colors and flavors, including cinnamon, licorice, and lemon. Start a collection.

Planting and Tending: Plant basil in full sun about a foot apart, and fertilize modestly throughout the growing season. Basil should receive regular water during the Central Texas summer. Once basil begins to put energy into flowers (the transition stage), it is no longer at its peak of flavor. You can have a long basil season by planting for succession.

Chives. Chives grow from bulblets and are in the allium family, as are onions. They are attractive plants for the front of a border or flower bed. Divide when they become overcrowded.

Planting and Tending: Plant clumps of chives in well-drained, average soil a couple of inches apart. They prefer full sun but will tolerate partial shade. Chives may deter several insect pests. Cut fresh leaves as desired.

Dill. This annual with delicate plumelike leaves likes full sun. It's a great larval food source for the eastern swallowtail butterfly.

Planting and Tending: Plant in full sun a foot or so apart. Dill grows best in well-drained soil. When it matures and the seeds turn brown, harvest; otherwise, it will seed randomly in your garden.

Fennel. This is a tall, bright green herb with airy foliage similar to that of dill. It can grow to 5 feet. It is also a good eastern swallowtail butterfly larval resource.

Planting and Tending: Plant seed in full sun a few feet apart. Fennel grows in average soil with good drainage. It needs moderate water.

Mint. There are many varieties and flavors of mint: peppermint and spearmint are the most popular, but pineapple, apple, and orange mint are also available. Mints take full sun and require frequent watering.

Planting and Tending: Mint is very aggressive! Planting it in a container will prevent it from taking over the garden. Harvest regularly to encourage new, more tender growth.

Oregano. This herb is popularly associated with Mediterranean dishes.

Planting and Tending: Plant in full sun in well-drained garden soil (it actually thrives in poor soil), and harvest when needed.

Parsley. Curled is the most popular parsley variety, but many cooks prefer the flat Italian. Both are readily available at garden centers. Parsley prefers cooler weather and is a great container plant. A true biennial, parsley will flower, go to seed, and die in its second year.

Planting and Tending: Parsley can be planted from seed, but it takes time and it's much easier to pick up a couple of 4-inch plants at the store. Plant in well-drained soil about 1 foot apart. Parsley prefers some shade and does well nestled next to larger plants.

Rosemary. This versatile herb is as welcome in the landscape as it is in the kitchen. Rosemary is available in upright or creeping habit and possesses attractive, dark green, needlelike foliage and a pungent fragrance. It is very heat tolerant and deer resistant. Rosemary withstands heavy trimming, and its branches can also be rooted by pegging them to the soil with garden staples. Although semihardy, it will suffer in a heavy frost.

Planting and Tending: Plant in dry, well-drained soil, and water minimally. Rosemary tolerates some shade but blooms best when grown in full sun.

Thyme. Delicate, woody stems covered by minute, fragrant leaves form a rapidly spreading lacework mat over the ground. Tiny lavender flowers appear in spring. There are many varieties of thyme to explore. Seeds germinate quickly. New plants may also be started from stem cuttings.

Planting and Tending: Plant a foot apart in any well-drained soil. It does best in full sun and takes a minimal amount of water.

Fruit

Backyard gardens generally are not the place for extensive fruit gardening. Most gardens are small, and most fruits take a lot of room. Our less than optimal environmental conditions may mean a lot of toil to bring in a sufficient crop. But Texas gardeners don't discourage easily and always seem up for a challenge and something new to try. Blackberries, if you have the space, can be grown quite easily; everyone wants to give strawberries a try.

Blackberries. Although blackberries require a fair amount of space, they adapt to a wide variety of soil and climatic conditions and are low-maintenance plants. Blackberries are biennial, which means that they put on vegetative growth the first year and produce fruit the following year. Plant 2 to 3 feet apart and in rows at least 10 feet apart. Prune out only producing canes after the harvest. New canes should be pinched back during the summer to encourage branching. Be sure to fertilize with a complete fertilizer and water well immediately after pruning. Blackberries have few pests except for birds stealing fruit. New varieties have an upright disposition and need no trellising.

RECOMMENDED VARIETIES
Arapaho: Thornless, productive
Brazos: Produces large fruit and is a good berry for cooking; has thorns
Brison: Has performed well on blackland clay; has thorns
Rosborough: Good for south-central Texas
Shawnee: Reportedly sweeter than Brazos

Strawberries. Our blistering summers are too harsh for strawberries, so treat them as annuals. Plant spring-bearing strawberries in the fall for a late spring harvest. They should be planted 18 inches apart in soil well prepared with compost and additional fertilizer. If your soil is mostly clay, it is best to plant in a raised bed filled with friable, well-drained soil. Strawberry plants must not be allowed to dry out; therefore, a polyethylene or straw mulch is absolutely necessary. Be on the lookout for pill bugs, slugs, snails (growing strawberries in strawberry pots helps prevent this pesky problem), and birds.

Recommended varieties: Obtaining the best varieties for Texas is often a challenge. Look for Chandler, Douglas, and Sequoia.

 **FYI: Vegetable Gardening**

Aggie Horticulture Garden ing Resources (http://aggie-horti-culture.tamu.edu/extension/gardening.html). Be sure to visit the links to Earth-Kind Gardening, a basic gardening guide with emphasis on environmental awareness and sponsored by Texas Co-operative Extension; and Texas Home Gardening Guide. The Easy Gardening Series provides a good basic introduction to growing our most popular vegetables.

The Essential Garden Guide (http://www.essentialgarden guide.com/). This elegant, attractive site treats all aspects of vegetable gardening from planning through harvest and storage. Planting dates may not be appropriate for Central Texas, but there is a wealth of useful information for all gardeners. Every vegetable is covered, from history of use, planting, and tending through harvest and storage.

National Sustainable Agriculture Information Service (http://attra.ncat.org/). User-friendly pest control locator and information. Created for the commercial producer, it has useful information for the home gardener, especially anyone interested in organic and sustainable gardening. This site contains good information on soils and compost publications and resources.

Texas Vegetable Crop Spring and Fall Planting Guides (http://plantanswers.tamu.edu/earth kind/ekgarden14.html). I rely heavily on Aggie Horticulture for vegetables because varieties and planting dates are crucial to successful gardening in Central Texas.

Vegetable Crop Guides from Texas Agricultural Extension Service
(http://aggie-horticulture. tamu.edu/extension/vegetable/ cropguides/). This no-frills, easy-to-use guide is a heavy favorite. Geared to commercial producers (fertilizer recommendations are in terms of acres) and certainly not slanted toward the organic (an amazing list of pesticides, most probably unavailable to the home gardener), it gives varieties, soil preference, optimum growing conditions, fertilization, irrigation, and pest management recommendations for each crop. Wonderful gems of information not commonly found in general gardening books are in the not-to-be-missed Comments/Production Keys sections. Hard copy is available.

Vegetable IPM, Texas A&M University Department of Entomology (http://vegipm.tamu.edu/ index.cfm). This well-organized site lists vegetables and their pests in a neat grid. Each pest has a text description at various life stages, photos of both insects and the damage they do, and a link to controls.

Trouble in the Garden

EEPER understanding of the environment and broader appreciation of how gardening practices can affect it have changed dramatically how we think about and deal with those things we don't want in our gardens—insects, diseases, and weeds. Our first impulse at the sight of an aphid or an ant is no longer to reach for the most lethal insect spray. As we have grown more aware of the importance of species diversity and the interconnection of living things, we have expanded our definition of gardening to include wildlife. We invite birds, butterflies, frogs, toads, lizards, and beneficial insects to participate in our gardening experience. We now know it is neither possible nor desirable

to eliminate all insects from our environment. Insects and plants evolved together. The vast majority of insects are either harmless or beneficial in our gardens. They are pollinators of our crops, decomposers of waste and debris, and a food source for much of life. They are as natural as can be.

A commonsense approach known as Integrated Pest Management (IPM) is a continuous method of pest control that does the least harm to people and the environment. It is promoted by extension agents, university researchers, and large agricultural producers. Empirical and effective, its emphasis is on management, not eradication.

Six Principles of Integrated Pest Management

1. Establishment of acceptable pest levels

2. Prevention

- Appropriate plant selection is key to a healthy garden or landscape. Flourishing native or well-adapted nonnative plants that thrive in our soils, heat, and humidity are plants that are more resis-

tant to disease and injury from pests than plants that have to struggle in an alien environment. Researching plants on the Internet is so easy that there is no excuse not to know any plant's basic requirements.

- Plant diversity promotes good garden health. Overuse of a single species (monoculture) can result in serious plant loss if infested by insects or infected by disease. Since insects and diseases often attack members of the same plant families, crop rotation is key to achieving healthy diversity in the vegetable garden.

3. Proper planting and maintenance

- When planting, set new plants in a hole at least twice as wide as the root ball. Set at ground level so that the top of the root ball is neither too high nor too low.
- Keep plants healthy with appropriate and consistent watering, fertilizing, and pruning. Opportunistic diseases get started when plants are weakened by

drought, heat stress, or nutrient depletion.

- Give plants plenty of space for adequate air circulation. Overcrowded conditions are an invitation to many fungal and bacterial diseases.
- Follow the manufacturer's instructions to ensure correct fertilizer application rate to avoid injury to plants.
- Weed and prune dead and damaged branches, which may harbor insects.
- Mulch to discourage weeds, retain moisture, and moderate soil temperature.

4. Sanitation

- We usually clean up the yard and garden for appearance first and the plants' well-being second, but clearing out old wood, leaves, and other debris that may harbor insects and disease can prevent much trouble down the road.
- Make sure watering cans, pots, and any other items that can collect water in the yard don't become magnets for breeding mosquitoes. Whenever possible, turn standing containers upside down.

- Discard diseased plants and weeds that have gone to seed in the trash. Compost piles often fail to heat up sufficiently to kill off seeds and disease organisms.

5. Observation

- Be sharp-eyed as you enjoy your garden. Leaves that are chewed, punctured, spotted, wilted, or distorted indicate the presence of insects or disease. (Of course, if you are butterfly gardening, these are welcome signs of success.) Be especially vigilant during rainy periods and when the temperature is moderate. These are great conditions for disease to take hold.
- Get into the habit of carrying pruning scissors to clip off diseased or invaded portions of plants. Frequent, keen-eyed tours of the garden will do much more than help you detect trouble. Your garden has much to teach, and there is so much to see—the succession of blossoms, developing fruit and seeds as the seasons move on, the enormous variety of living things and their relationships to one another.

6. Intervention and control

- Manual control methods include handpicking as an effective way to deal with weeds early in the season before they become rampant and with the larger, slower, critters such as snails and slugs. Pluck out diseased flowers and vegetable plants before others are infected. Repeated sharp jets of water in the direction of an aphid-infested plant can be a sufficient check if the population has not gotten out of control.

- Biological control is the use of predators, parasites, fungi, viruses, and growth-hormone regulators to suppress those we consider pests in our gardens. The release of praying mantises or ladybugs is a good example of biological control. Some experts consider its effectiveness in the home garden dubious. It's great fun for children to witness the hatchlings emerge from the egg case, but the released insects' first bite to eat is usually a sibling, and others are quick to scatter beyond the boundary of a suburban lot. Life stages of predator and prey may be out of sync. Ladybugs for sale in plastic mesh bags at the garden center are often nonnative species and, having had their natural life cycle interrupted, are seldom robust. In a diverse and balanced garden the best biological control is in progress all the time as hunter and hunted live out their lives.

Anole on guard

Chemical control may be necessary when problems become too widespread or beyond cultural and manual methods. Research has cast serious concern, if not iron-clad evidence, about the safety (especially for children) of many products once considered standard issue in our garden arsenals. Chlordane and Dursban have been banned or their use restricted in the home garden. Today most nurseries and home-improvement centers offer "soft pesticides," nonpersistent products made from natural sources, as alternatives to broad-spectrum, synthetic pesticides. Biorationals, whose active ingredient may be bacteria, viruses, fungi, or protozoa, are target specific and do no harm to other organisms. *Bacillus thuringiensis* (Bt), a bacterial disease, is a commonly used biological control for insect larvae, such as caterpillars, but not for adult insects. To be effective, it must be ingested in sufficient quantities to paralyze the digestive system of the larvae. Since Bt does not distinguish between the larva of a monarch butterfly and a tomato hornworm, it should not be used in your butterfly garden.

Pesticide Basics

Pesticides come in many forms: liquids, dusts, sprays, and granules. Dusts and granules can be applied directly to the problem; sprays are sold as wettable powders, flowable formulations, or oil or emulsifiable concentrates and need to be mixed with water before use. Pesticides can be formulated in multipurpose combinations (chemicals sold for rose care often contain a fungicide, an insecticide, and a miticide all in one). Many common insecticides are broad-spectrum, effective against an array of pests; some are targeted at specific insects or insect families. Some insecticides kill on contact; others, referred to as systemics, are absorbed by roots, stems, or leaves and carried by sap throughout the plant, killing pests that feed on the treated plants. Systemic insecticides tend to be longer lasting than those that kill on contact. Systemics are especially effective for sucking insects. Do not use systemic pesticides on plants you intend to eat.

Mixing. When mixing pesticides, use measuring utensils dedicated to that use only. Do not borrow from the kitchen! Mix up only the needed amount, and always clean the utensils after

use. This is especially important if you use the same utensil for insecticides, fungicides, and herbicides, which are not always compatible.

Storing. Store pesticides in their original containers in a dry, well-ventilated space away from children, pets, and food. Never remove the labels, and keep the containers securely closed. Liquid pesticides must not be allowed to freeze. Since some pesticides lose their potency over time, it's a good idea to check the label for expiration dates. Do not buy in quantities larger than you require, even if they are a bargain. The point is to use up the product and avoid the problem of disposal.

Applying. Before applying chemicals, remove all toys, pet dishes, and other items from the area that family members or pets may touch. Choose a calm morning, without rain in the forecast. Should a breeze pick up, be sure to be upwind to avoid inhaling the pesticide. Because some pesticides can irritate skin and/or eyes, it's a good idea to wear long-sleeved and long-legged clothing and goggles. It is best to apply pesticides when the temperature is below 85°F. Always completely cover the tops and undersides of all leaves.

Organic Gardening. Organic gardeners seeking help in controlling insect pests chemically should look for the OMRI label. These products have been reviewed and approved by the Organic Materials Review Institute, a national nonprofit organization composed of representatives of the organic industry.

- **Diatomaceous earth** is a nontoxic, fine powder made from diatoms, a common type of phytoplankton. It is very effective on many ground crawlers, such as pill bugs and slugs. It pierces their shells or soft bodies with its fine particles. Take precautions against inhaling any powder or dusting product you may use in the garden.
- **Sulfur** is effective on powdery mildew and spider mites but may stain buildings and walls and should not be used in temperatures greater than 85°F.
- **Insecticidal soaps** work by smothering insects. Some plants do not tolerate insecticidal soap, so always test on a small area before applying to the whole plant. To get good coverage, spray both sides of the plant leaves. After the insects have been killed, rinse the soap residue from the plant with a spray of water.
- **Rotenone and pyrethrins** are nonpersistent insecticides made from toxic plant products. They are useful against whiteflies, aphids, and small caterpillars. Both are toxic to fish and other aquatic life.

READ THE LABEL

All chemicals, fertilizers or pesticides, should be used *only* according to label instructions. A quick way to determine a pesticide's toxicity level is to look for the words CAUTION (lowest level), WARNING (moderate toxicity), and DANGER (highest toxicity). These designations are required by law and are present on every pesticide product. Be sure to read the storage and disposal instructions and the danger to the environment. Fish and other aquatic life are very sensitive to chemicals. Take time to read the small-print information, which is often ingeniously located under the main label and difficult to access.

FYI: Pesticides

Organic Materials Review Institute (http://www.omri.org/) is a national nonprofit organization that determines which products are allowed for use in organic production and processing. OMRI-listed—or approved— products may be used on operations that are certified organic under the USDA National Organic Program.

Pesticide Profiles (http://ace. ace.orst.edu/info/extoxnet/pips/ searchindex.html), maintained cooperatively by University of California–Davis, Oregon State University, Michigan State University, and Cornell University, offers the most comprehensive, hard-to-get, up-to-date information on pesticides. Although the information is more technical than many gardeners require, most lingering questions about the safety of individual chemicals will be answered here.

Aphids and ladybug larvae on tropical milkweed

Common Insect Pests of Central Texas

Aphids. Many species of aphids (more than thirteen hundred in North America) in an array of colors and life stages attack our flowers, vegetables, and landscape plants. They injure by sucking plant juices. Often they can be controlled with repeated water hosings or applications of a diluted soap-and-water mixture, but you need to be diligent to stay on top of the situation. Ladybugs and other predators may take care of some. Some species have become resistant to chemical pesticides, which also may eliminate the aphids' natural predators.

Caterpillars. These insects are a challenge for the butterfly gardener. Since many caterpil-

LEARN YOUR BUGS!

There are thousands of insects, but only a small percentage of them cause serious trouble in the garden. Many are beautiful and important to maintaining or improving species diversity. Dragonflies and damselflies are voracious predators of other insects, especially mosquitoes. Many beetle species feed on other insects and their eggs. We all know the ladybug, but few of us can identify its larval, and even hungrier, form. The lovely, delicate lacewing feeds on aphids and mealybugs. Bugs bring birds to the garden.

lars grow into butterflies, you need to identify the culprit and handpick or consider tolerating the damage. Tent caterpillars or webworms can engulf entire tree limbs in massive webs. In limited numbers, they are more unsightly than damaging. Grackles and other birds can be your first line of defense, or you can prune out affected areas before the caterpillars hatch. If the mass of webworms is located at a workable height, puncture the web with a pole saw or other sharp object to allow penetration and spray with Bt, available under the names Dipel and Thuricide. Although tent caterpillars infest a variety of hosts, pecan and mulberry

Webworms

trees are particularly susceptible. Several caterpillars make up the group known as cabbageworms or loopers. These pests can do a lot of damage in the vegetable garden. Members of the *Brassica* genus (broccoli, cabbage, cauliflower, kale) are all susceptible, especially when newly planted. Sheltering young plants under row cover is helpful. Fortunately, many caterpillars are easy to see and handpick.

Fire Ants. Imported from South America, these pests with their stinging, venomous bite are at the top of the Most Unwanted List. Decades-long use of broad-spectrum pesticides to control them has yielded little success. Less harmful to the environment, baits such as Amdro and Ascend kill the queens before they leave the nest to establish new colonies. Award and Logic reduce the production of viable eggs, eventually leading to fewer fire ants, but colonies may remain active for months after treatment. Organic gardeners can use boiling water, trail barriers made from talcum powder or diatomaceous earth, and baits containing abamectin or spinosad. Weather, time of year, time of day, and size of infestation all play a part in the efficacy of various control measures.

Harlequin Bugs. These insects, easily identified by their shield-like back with red, yellow, and orange markings, attack many vegetable varieties. The insects relentlessly suck the life out of asparagus, beans, corn, okra, squash, tomatoes, and members of the cabbage family. Remaining active throughout the mild winters of the Gulf states, they may produce two to four generations in a season. If the invaded vegetables are nearing the end of production, remove plants to prevent the harlequin bugs from spreading throughout the garden.

Leaf-footed Bugs. These insects are dark brown with a whitish-yellowish stripe across the central part of the back. The hind legs have signature flattened, leaflike expansions from which the insect gets its name. Beans, black-eyed peas, sorghum, and tomatoes are likely victims. These insects also feed on the stems and tender leaves of potatoes.

Mealybugs. Highly visible white, cottony webs on the leaves and stems are the telltale sign of mealybugs. Mealybugs belong to the scale family of insects and like a warm, moist climate. They feed on plant sap. They favor house plants and in the garden are attracted to cacti, citrus, coleus, and gardenias. Small populations seldom do much damage and can be removed with a jet of water from the hose or with an application of alcohol with a cotton swab. Larger populations can cause leaf drop and may be controlled with insecticidal soap or other pesticides.

Nematodes. These microscopic worms live mostly in the soil. There are many, many species. Some are predatory and help control other garden pests such as cutworms; others, like the root-knot nematode that thrives in hot, dry soil, cause enormous horticultural and agricultural damage worldwide. Many ornamentals are susceptible, especially boxwood, fig, gardenia, and passionflower, as well as chrysanthemums and other annuals. In vegetable gardens, okra and tomatoes are threatened. Affected plants lose color, appear stunted, and may gradually die. Diseased plants have swollen and noded roots, or brown or black spots or streaks on the roots. Because many nematicides also kill other insects, earthworms, and plants, be sure to read carefully the manufacturer's instructions when selecting

a chemical control. An alternative in the vegetable garden is to plant a cover crop of cereal (Elbon) rye in winter. Trapped in the roots of the rye, the nematodes will die. In spring, turn the rye into the soil. It is a wonderful fertilizer.

Red Spider Mites. Fine webs on plants tell you that spider mites are at work. You can just barely see these small invaders on the undersides of leaves of junipers, marigolds, roses, and tomatoes during the hotter, drier months. Spider mites are notoriously persistent and difficult to control. The most effective control for infestation in annuals is the removal of affected plants. A good first try at getting rid of spider mites is a thorough shower from a high-pressure sprayer. A summer horticultural oil (2 percent) and insecticidal soaps are also recommended for other plants.

Scale. Masses of green, brown, or purple dots, usually found on the undersides of leaves but sometimes on stems and fruits, indicate the presence of scale. These hard-shelled insects weaken plants by sucking plant juices. Common susceptible host plants are camellia and hibiscus (both of which suffer from white scale), euonymus, gardenia, and jasmine. To control, spray with a garden-type oil emulsion in the spring or fall, when the temperature has been below 85°F and above 45°F for at least a week.

Snails and Slugs. These are easy to see and much slower than you are, so handpick or give beer traps (shallow pans or jar tops filled with stale beer and sunk into the soil at ground level) a chance before resorting to chemical controls.

Sow Bugs, or Pill Bugs. These dark gray, fat, hard-shelled bugs feed on decaying organic matter. They do little damage to healthy, growing plants but can be attracted to dead or injured tissue. Since they prefer dark, moist places, they can be discouraged with good garden sanitation and by pulling back mulch a couple of inches from the base or crown of plants. They will flock to overturned grapefruit rinds set out in the evening, which you can collect in the morning and discard. Diatomaceous earth, too, is an effective control on dry soil.

Squash Bugs. Similar in appearance to leaf-footed bugs and stink bugs, squash bugs like to hide out at the base of plants in the squash family in hot weather, eating stems and leaves. Prevention is possible by keeping the base of squash plants free of mulch.

Stink Bugs. This large family of shield-shaped bugs injures plants by sucking sap from blossoms, buds, and fruit. The **Southern Green Stink Bug** likes just about all vegetables. They are not very quick, so if you just have a few, handpicking is effective. Pyrethrins and insecticidal soaps are also effective.

Thrips. These tiny, winged, sucking insects cause streaked foliage, partial opening of flowers, and brown edges on petals. A major problem on roses and onions, they are difficult to control with chemicals. Good garden sanitation is an important prevention measure.

Whiteflies. It's the wingless larvae (resemble scale insects) of whiteflies that do the damage. They weaken plants by sucking the juices of many flowering plants and some vegetables. They also excrete a telltale sticky honeydew on the leaves, which in turn supports a black fungal growth. A good shot with the

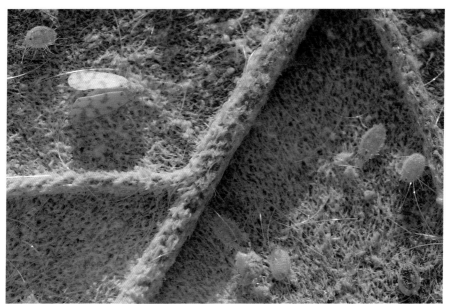

Whitefly larvae and adults

hose should get rid of them. Control of adults may require a pesticide.

 **FYI: Insects**

Texas A & M Department of Entomology (http://insects.tamu .edu/extension/insctans/). Insect identification, fun facts, insect damage, and control information are just a few useful and enlightening topics available on this site. Visit the outstanding photographs, video, and audio features.

Texas Imported Fire Ant Research and Management Project

(http://fireant.tamu.edu/). Probably the best research-based information on control of fire ants available. Especially helpful is the tab to "Managing Fire Ants," which includes discussion of speed, application rate, best season for application, and toxicity level.

Common Diseases

Diseases can be very difficult for the home gardener to diagnose and treat because so many symptoms appear similar. A well-trained eye is often necessary to distinguish a bacterial problem from a fungal or viral problem. Many disease troubles can be avoided with appropriate plant selection and good cultural practices. Because diseases thrive in humid conditions, it is important to provide adequate space for good air circulation. Many problems are best treated by pruning out and properly discarding affected areas, or in the case of flowers or vegetables, simply removing the diseased plants. Following are some of the more common disease problems encountered in the garden.

Botrytis Blight. Present in most soils and thriving in moist, cool conditions, the fungi infect many flowers, shrubs, trees, and vegetables. They cause spotting and decay on leaves, flowers, and fruit of affected plants. Cut out affected plant parts in trees and shrubs; remove entire flower and vegetable plants.

Canker. This is a collection of plant diseases caused by fungi, bacteria, and viruses. Symptoms include dead tissue that grows slowly. Some cause little damage, while others may be devastating. Some are treatable; others are not. Ash, mulberry, oak, and roses are susceptible.

Chlorosis. A condition most commonly caused by an iron deficiency in the soil or the alkaline nature of the soil, chlorosis prevents plants from being able to use iron. This is the demon of many popular acid-loving plants, such as azaleas, camellias, and gardenias. The leaves will turn yellow, but the veins remain green. Chlorosis can be prevented by incorporating plenty of peat moss when planting acid-loving plants and corrected with applications of iron chelate. Chlorosis can also occur in lawns. Many lawn fertilizers formulated for Central Texas contain iron to prevent this condition.

Cotton Root Rot. This is a soil-borne disease that suddenly kills seemingly healthy plants. It is most likely to occur from June to frost; plants suffering from heat and drought are most vulnerable. Leaves on trees (and other plants) turn yellow because of the deteriorating root systems. This, however, is also symptomatic of other problems, including improper watering. Plants are easily removed from the soil, revealing roots covered with a yellow or brown growth. Unfortunately, no current fungicide has proven effective in controlling the disease. The best prevention is to buy plants that are moderately to highly resistant to the disease. These include bald cypress, boxwood, cedar elm, crape myrtle, holly, honeysuckle, juniper, live oak, pecan, pyracantha, redbud, red cedar, red oak, and sycamore. Trees and plants that are most susceptible are apple, cottonwood, elm (*not* cedar elm), fruitless mulberry, ligustrum, loquat, roses, and silver maple.

Damping-Off. This fungal disease attacks seeds and seedlings. Seeds may fail to germinate, or the stems at the soil surface show symptoms of rotting. It occurs most often in cold, wet, or compacted soil. Preventive measures are good sanitation practices, use of well-decomposed compost (green compost can promote damping-off), and good drainage. Plant when the soil temperature is warm enough to encourage fast germination and growth.

Fire Blight. Symptoms of fire blight are easily identified: branch tips die back, giving the affected limbs a scorched, burned appearance. Once the symptoms appear, pruning out affected branches can help prevent the spread of the disease. There is, however, no guaranteed cure. Tools must be cleaned with a chlorine solution between cuts

to avoid spreading the disease. Apples, pears, cotoneaster, Indian hawthorn, loquat, pyracantha, photinia, and quince are susceptible.

Leaf Spot (bacterial and fungal). Many leaf-spotting fungi and bacteria cause only cosmetic damage and are no cause for alarm or treatment. You will notice that leaf spots are most severe in mild, wet weather. The fungal leaf spot disease *Entomosporium maculatum* has been a serious threat to red-tip photinia in Central Texas. The long-term prognosis for affected plants, even with fungicide applications, is not good. Practice good hygiene to prevent spreading the disease to other plants. It may be best to remove the plant and replace it with another species. Collect and discard all fallen leaves. Be careful watering lawns or beds in the vicinity of photinia to avoid prolonged periods when leaves are wet. Black spot is a fungal disease that is very common in roses grown in Central Texas.

Oak Wilt. This fungal disease is a major problem for live oaks, Shumard oaks, and Spanish oaks in some Central Texas neighborhoods. Species of red oaks are especially hard hit, often dying within weeks of detection. The symptoms vary according to species. In live oaks, the leaf veins remain green as the area between veins turns light green to yellow. On red oaks and blackjack oaks, leaves turn a reddish brown, and wilting proceeds inward from the tips. The leaves will remain on the tree for a brief time after tree death. The disease is transmitted through the roots and by sap-feeding beetles that carry the fungal spores. Because stacked firewood from susceptible species can aid in the spread of the disease, cover any questionable firewood pile with clear plastic, tucking the edges of the plastic cover into the ground to prevent insect infestation. Avoid pruning oaks between mid-January and mid-June, when the fungus-spreading beetle is most active. It is recommended that pruning cuts on susceptible varieties be painted with a wound paint. Trenching to separate root systems should be dealt with on a neighborhood level. Many neighborhood associations and municipal governments are prepared to assist should there be an oak wilt outbreak in your area. Your county extension agent is an excellent source of information.

Powdery Mildew. One of the most common fungal diseases, powdery mildew appears as white or gray mold on the leaves, eventually turning them yellow. Unlike many other fungi, powdery mildew affects dry as well as wet leaves. Crape myrtles (especially the older varieties) and euonymus commonly fall victim. Buy resistant varieties.

FYI: Diseases

University of California Statewide Integrated Pest Management Program (http://www.ipm.ucdavis.edu/PMG/menu.homegarden.html) is superbly organized and has excellent photos, particularly of pests and diseases.

Weeds

Weeds, of course, are just unwanted plants or plants in the wrong place. The charming blue dayflower (*Commelina erecta*) so admired on a walk in the woods becomes a tenacious enemy in the flower or vegetable bed. A number of pesky broad-leaved weeds, grasses, and sedges bedevil garden beds and longed-for perfect lawns. Here, prevention is the easiest and most effective control. Weeds cannot run, hop, or fly away from you. Watch for them, and pull them out early and often. Keep lawns healthy and beds mulched.

Weed Control Products

Corn gluten meal (a by-product of the corn milling process) was discovered to work as an organic preemergent herbicide on turf weeds. The key to corn gluten effectiveness is timing. Corn gluten must be applied when weed seeds are sprouting to be an effective weed killer. Water in the initial application, and then allow for a drying period to complete the process. Corn gluten may be used in the garden also.

Glyphosate (Roundup, Rodeo) is a nonselective broad herbicide that interrupts the plant's metabolism. Many prefer it as a weed and grass killer because it must make contact with growing, green foliage to kill and does not move into the soil and endanger neighboring plants. It will, however, kill plants that may have been sprayed accidentally or from wind drift.

Sedgehammer and **Image** are selective postemergent herbicides for the control of nutsedges, noxious weeds that defy other herbicides. When applied as directed, they will not harm bermudagrass, St. Augustine, or zoysiagrass. Nutsedges are difficult to eradicate by digging up because the nutlets break off easily and reemerge later.

Vinegar (20 percent; for comparison, culinary vinegar is 5 percent) is an organic weed control that works well in the fall. It is nonselective, so you have to be careful when using it. Depending on the brand, it may contain other organic products such as citrus oil and molasses or other oils that perform as sticking agents.

 **FYI: Weeds**

City of Austin's Grow Green Weed Landscape Problems (http://www.ci.austin.tx.us/growgreen/). Click on "Landscape Problems" and then "Weeds" to download a superb PDF version of the weed control fact sheet, which covers all topics of weed control in the home landscape. There are excellent photos for identification, a variety of control tactics, toxicity levels of herbicides, and additional references.

Mockingbird damage on tomatoes

Other Causes of Damage in the Garden, or "Oh, Deer"

Insects, diseases, and weeds are not the only challenges you will face in the garden. Deer have their preferences in lush, good times, but when conditions are bad, few plants are safe. The list of sworn-by repellents is long; the list of *deer-proof* plants is short. Repellents include blood meal, human hair, and coyote urine spray. In addition to indifferent results, most are easily washed away by rain and require repeated applications. They work best when plant life is flourishing and abundant and the deer have many choices. When not, few repellents will work. Cast iron plant, crimson barberry, Mexican oregano, pampas grass, red yucca, the salvia 'Indigo Spires,' and Texas sage or cenizo are reputed to be deer-proof. Strong-smelling plants, such as lantana, juniper, and rosemary are considered to have good deer resistance. Physical barriers like fences and polyurethane mesh provide the best protection.

Two favorite Web sites are listed in the FYI section.

Pets and visiting wildlife can also take their toll. Armadillos looking for grubs and worms can tear up a lawn and uproot a flower or vegetable garden overnight. Trapping is helpful, but there are no guarantees against return visits. Squirrels are pests in the vegetable garden. They are also active diggers in fall, just in time for spring-blooming bulb planting. A layer of chicken wire placed over the bulbs will discourage the squirrels. The bulbs will grow right through the wire and be fine. Even our beloved Texas state bird, the mockingbird, is a major menace to ripening tomatoes.

 **FYI: Deer**

Camouflage Gardening (http://www.npsot.org/plant_lists/deer_resistant.html). This popular list compiled by Patti Simons, aka the Deer Lady, with the aid of others, is a work in progress. Simons's approach to deer problems is "camouflage gardening," or the use of plants that are unappealing to deer to confuse and distract.

Deer in the Urban Landscape (http://aggie-horticulture.tamu edu/plantanswers/publications/deerbest.html). Forrest W. Appleton, retired certified nursery professional and Bexar County Master Gardener, shares his personal list of deer-resistant plants.

Mechanical, Chemical, and Environmental Damage

Trees are especially vulnerable to damage during construction. Soil is compacted, roots are severed, and trunks and branches get bashed and broken. Grade change and use of fill can be devastating to trees; often the results are not visible until years later. Casually wielded mowers, edgers, and weed whackers take their toll on plants and user alike.

Applications of the wrong pesticide or fertilizer or in the wrong amount can damage or kill plants.

Drought, extreme heat and cold, wind, and untimely changes in weather are all stressful. When trying to diagnose an ailing plant, consider if any other of these nonorganic events may have occurred.

Sometimes even the best attempts to keep plants healthy can fail. Determining what is wrong is not simple, and curing can be even more complicated. Even nursery staff and plant experts may disagree or may not be able to give advice in time to save the patient. Gardeners, always philosophical, should view these times as opportunities for new plants and new ideas.

Index